MARKETING FINANCIAL ADVISORY SERVICES

MARKETING FINANCIAL ADVISORY SERVICES

A Hands-On Guide

JEFFREY L. SEGLIN

PRENTICE HALL, Englewood Cliffs, New Jersey   07632

Library of Congress Cataloging-in-Publication Data

Seglin, Jeffrey L.
  Marketing financial advisory services.

  Bibliography; p.
  Includes index.
  1. Financial planners—Marketing. I. Title.
HG179.5.S44   1988   332.6′2   88-5803
ISBN 0-13-558578-3

Editorial/production supervision: Editing, Design & Production, Inc.
Cover design: Lundgren Graphics, Ltd.
Manufacturing buyer: Edward O'Dougherty

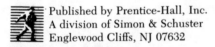 Published by Prentice-Hall, Inc.
A division of Simon & Schuster
Englewood Cliffs, NJ 07632

The publisher offers discounts on this book when ordered in bulk quantities. For more information, write:
  Special Sales/College Marketing
  Prentice Hall
  College Technical and Reference Division
  Englewood Cliffs, NJ 07632

Printed in the United States of America

10 9 8 7 6 5 4 3 2 1

ISBN 0-13-558578-3

PRENTICE-HALL INTERNATIONAL (UK) LIMITED, *London*
PRENTICE-HALL OF AUSTRALIA PTY, LIMITED, *Sydney*
PRENTICE-HALL CANADA, INC., *Toronto*
PRENTICE-HALL HISPANOAMERICANA, S.A., *Mexico*
PRENTICE-HALL OF INDIA PRIVATE LIMITED, *New Delhi*
PRENTICE-HALL OF JAPAN, INC., *Tokyo*
SIMON & SCHUSTER ASIA PTE., LTD., *Singapore*
EDITORA PRENTICE-HALL DO BRASIL, LTDA, *Rio de Janeiro*

To Nancy,
Whose love has shown me the triumph of hope over experience.

CONTENTS

PREFACE

More than four years ago, I began covering the financial planning beat. I had already been writing on personal finance, small business, and banking, areas that I still cover. But four years ago, I entered a world that was made up of a smorgasbord of financial services professionals: insurance agents, accountants, stockbrokers, bankers, registered investment advisors, money managers, and virtually every group that fits into the category of financial services professionals.

While this vast array of expertise can bring exciting insights to a young profession, it sometimes also brings confusion. Financial advisors (or "financial planners" as the industry organizations have come to call their members) must recognize their strengths and rely either on a strong network of other professionals or, in the case of some of the more ambitious planners, an in-house staff with expertise in tax planning, insurance planning, education planning, investment planning, retirement planning, and estate planning.

What has too often happened, particularly in the one-person shop, where an independent financial advisor sets out to capture a share of a market hungry for advice, is that, zealous to build a successful practice, the planner ignores the very basics that are being sold to prospective clients—planning. While, of course, this varies from advisor to advisor, many professionals who are the sole proprietors of a business have no well-thought-out business plan. Yes, they do marketing. But too often they do so in a shotgun manner, responding only to an immediate need in their marketplace.

Many financial services professionals, unless they are with a large organization that has its own in-house marketing and corporate communications department, simply do not have the time to focus on marketing issues without taking a chunk out of the time they have to devote to clients.

The studies in *Marketing Financial Advisory Services* give the professional financial advisor, whether working alone or in a large organization, the techniques that have proven successful for others in the financial services profession, whether bankers, accountants, insurance agents, or fee-only financial advisors. The book is divided into five parts:

1. product or service development
2. product or service differentiation
3. target marketing
4. product or service presentation
5. selling techniques

Within each part are chapters that illustrate how professionals have successfully experimented with a variety of marketing techniques to find the one that works for their practice.

The book follows a logical progession. First the product or service is established. Then it is differentiated, made to stand out from the crowd. Next, a target market is established. After the business is firmly on its feet, various methods of presentation, from advertising and creating a corporate image to using newsletters and serving as a media source, are explored. Finally, techniques of pricing and selling services and building the mature practice are studied. The result is a journey through the business practices of successful financial advisors.

At the end of the book is a section called Resources, which lists the names, addresses, and phone numbers of service providers mentioned in the book that the reader may wish to contact. A bibliography lists books and articles covering areas the reader might want to pursue further.

Since the early 1970s, financial planning has been growing as an "industry." More and more financial services professionals have recognized the attractiveness of adding advice and planning to the services they already offered. For the accountant, it means adding more business to the tax planning he or she has already been doing for years. For the insurance agent or stockbroker, it presents opportunities to combine planning with selling products. For the banker, it presents the opportunity to establish the strong relationship with the customer that results in a long-term use of bank products and services.

With the introduction of money market funds in the 1970s, the incredible growth in popularity of other types of mutual funds in the 1980s bull market, and the confusion caused by the stock market tumble in October 1987, consumers have eagerly sought the advice of financial professionals. Too often, the professional has rushed to serve these consumers without clearly defining his or her market or establishing a marketing plan to attract the desired clientele. What, unfortunately, has also happened is unfavorable press attention to those who have seen an opportunity to take advantage of a public hungry for knowledge. The sins of these few have tarnished the image of the many ethical, legitimate professionals who work hard to keep their businesses going. It is an unfortunate occurrence, but one that is unlikely to go away.

There are no magic guarantees for success in the financial services marketplace. But there are basic marketing strategies that have worked for years in other professional fields, that can also be applied in this market. *Marketing Financial Advisory Services* is a study of what's working in the marketplace and how you can use successful examples as models for your own professional practice.

The strategies and techniques in *Marketing Financial Advisory Services* give the professional the tools he or she needs to succeed in a competitive marketplace. The book shows how to attract and build a loyal client base using both innovation and common sense. Coupled with appropriate training in a financial services profession and a commitment to serving the needs of the client while fully disclosing the risks or potential conflicts of interest involved with a recommended investment or strategy, these marketing techniques can give the professional the edge needed to succeed in the financial services marketplace. What's here is what has worked in marketing financial advisory services.

Samuel Johnson wrote: "No man I suppose leaps at once into deep water who does not know how to swim." *Marketing Financial Advisory Services* teaches you the strokes you must know to keep from drowning in the competitive marketplace. It teaches you the marketing strategies you need to be among the best in the business.

Jeffrey L. Seglin

ACKNOWLEDGMENTS

Marketing Financial Advisory Services is the result of more than two years of interviews with financial services professionals. Many people were instrumental in helping to develop what has become the final version of this book. The people who are mentioned in the various chapters were gracious enough to tolerate my intrusions and helpful in providing professional insight.

When I approached Bob Veres and Jack Lange, editor and editor-in-chief of *Financial Planning* magazine, with the idea of exploring selling and marketing within the financial services profession, they provided encouragement and advice that have gone well beyond expectations. I am grateful for the advice and friendship they have extended to me. Suzanne Paola, formerly a senior editor at *Financial Planning* and now pursuing creative writing as a fellowship student at the University of Virginia, did much to help shape the chapters and suggest areas that should be covered in this book.

John Waggoner, Bob Clark, Matthew Rovner, Joan Miller, Peter Harrington, Joan Schneider, Ken Grange, Richard Bevilacqua, Jennifer Suydam, and Linda McKinney were all helpful in guiding me to good sources of information. Cary Purvis, managing editor of *Financial Planning*, has been a joy to work with and an endless source of support and encouragement.

Jeffrey Krames, my editor at Prentice-Hall, was enthusiastic about the project from the first time I mentioned it to him at the annual convention of the International Association for Financial Planning in Chicago. His support has never waned. Kate Bradford of Editing, Design & Production, Inc. did a wonderful job of fine-tuning the manuscript.

My stepdaughter, Bethany, who is just about to enter college, reminded me—through her help, caring, and sense of humor—that there are times when it is best to put work aside. My stepson, Eddie, who is now in college, spent one summer researching articles, running errands, answering the phone, and generally keeping my work life more sane so there was time to do the research and interviews necessary for this book. Loren and Lisa Gary have steadfastly made my life easier while I was writing this book.

Evan Marshall, my agent and friend, has been unflagging in his support of this and all of my projects. When my writing of the manuscript stalled, Evan, on more than one occasion, got me back on track and focused.

The two best sounding boards I had for the final book were Jim Lewis and Nancy Seglin. Jim, in addition to being my best friend and one of the finer writer/editor/humorists I know, has taken time and care in helping me shape the final manuscript and given up many Sunday evenings talking to me long-distance about ideas he had for strengthening the book. Nancy's expertise as a book editor is only surpassed by the love and support she has given me and the patience she has shown living with me while I worked on this project.

PART ONE
A PRODUCT IS BORN

There is a challenge to every financial services professional who attempts to bring a product or service to market. That challenge is one of determining what the best product is to meet the needs of the consumer. Intertwined in that decision-making process are elements of market research, quality control, competitive analysis, and a score of other techniques that lay the groundwork for the successful introduction of a product to the marketplace. The four chapters in Part One look at four distinct attempts to enter the financial services marketplace with products or services.

Chapter 1 explores how The New England, a Boston-based financial services company, launched its national network of financial planning shops, called New England Financial Advisors (NEFA), after many months of market research and a pilot group study conducted among some of its general agencies around the country. The process of creating an organization of somewhat autonomous yet affiliated agents was not without problems. Compensation, commission structure, software, regulatory issues, and other complexities of managing a national financial planning service had to be wrestled with. Chapter 1 looks at how The New England's home office management created a forum for shared ideas among its NEFA participants and how it attempted an ambitious national rollout of a new service that could be offered by its general agents in the field.

Where Chapter 1 describes how a massive financial services organization entered the financial planning arena, Chapter 2 explores how two planners, Jeffrey Barefoot and Thomas Hart, both former certified public accountants (CPAs), set up shop. The interesting twist is that these two former CPAs both worked for one of the NEFA shops that The New England had just gotten off the ground. Not only did The First Continental Company have to confront all of the issues typical for a startup venture (such as market identification, pricing, and guarantees); it also had the chore of figuring out how to make it alone without giving the appearance of stealing clients away from its former NEFA home. Chapter 2 looks at what happens when the rules of the game change so much at an organization that some of the players are motivated to change fields—to capitalize on that entrepreneurial flame burning inside them, convincing them that they could be flourishing as owners rather than slaving as employees.

Chapter 3 examines how Gerald Mueller and James Breznay used the input and ideas of financial advisors when they launched the first federally chartered bank in Massachusetts in more than two decades. Instead of the traditional bricks-and-mortar approach most banks use, New England Federal Savings Bank uses telemarketing, automated teller machines, direct mail, and newspaper space advertisements as the keys to its marketing game plan. The result? A high-tech, high-service approach to banking that, while not threatening the stability of the behemoth Boston banks, is a successful entry into the market that exceeded expectations.

Chapter 4 shows how Ken Peterson, chairman of Financial Equity Group in Birmingham, Michigan, worked with Merle Harmon's Fan Fair, a midwestern chain of speciality retailers, to meet the needs of broker-dealers hungry for a product that stressed economics over tax breaks. At a time when oil and gas prices faltered and tax reform cut many benefits of traditional tax-shelter products, the drive was on to find new investment vehicles that broker-dealers could sell to their affluent investors. Peterson saw the opportunity for a new breed of investment and capitalized on the market need by introducing limited partnership offerings in a chain of stores that offered sports-team–related products to sports fans. Chapter 4 also shows how Peterson taught his prospective broker-dealers about retailing and franchising, both foreign territories for professionals who had been immersed in oil and gas and real estate products for years.

All of the chapters in part I show how successful financial services professionals were able to develop a marketable product or service. By meeting market demand with a product or service developed with sophisticated market research and economic sense, these professionals were able to give birth to financial products and services that had the potential to capture a significant share of the desired marketplace.

4

1 STRENGTH IN NUMBERS . . . BIG NUMBERS: *The Development of a National Force of Financial Planners*

"First off, the most important piece of marketing is creating a forum to share the best ideas of what's working in financial planning as well as the pitfalls. That's the way we do business in life insurance and equities, and that's the way we'll do it in financial planning." Jim Zilinski, The New England's senior vice president of financial services marketing, is clearheaded on the matter. For a year and a half (ending in June 1985), The New England (formerly called New England Mutual Life Insurance Company) solicited opinions from selected members of its field force as part of a joint venture designed to figure out the best way to offer personal financial planning.

The result was NEFA (pronounced knee-fah), New England Financial Advisors, an opportunity for The New England's life insurance agents and registered representatives—who sell securities through New England Securities Corporation—to get into financial planning in a big way quickly without, as David Plotkin, equities manager with the northern California NEFA office, put it, "having to mortgage our firstborn male child."

NATIONAL UMBRELLA =
ECONOMIES OF SCALE

From a marketing standpoint, NEFA offers many advantages to a small agency of perhaps twenty-five or thirty agents. The chief advantage is economy of scale. Computer hardware and software can be purchased in bulk by the national office. Ad slicks can be done up in volume and supplied to individual NEFA operators. The home office's national ad campaign, which rolled out in the trade press in August 1985 and in the consumer press the following December, brought exposure for all NEFA shops.

"They're getting the benefit of the mass buying power of a large corporation," Zilinski says. "If they were to go out and buy the software alone, it would cost them more than the first-year NEFA fee."

The fees are reasonable. There are three options the NEFA rep can choose from in deciding what kind of financial planning to offer. The first is the most basic. Says Stephanie Brown, president of NEFA: "Organizations that don't have a local practice now can affiliate with the home office, where the plan will be done. The planner does the data gathering, plan presentation, and the ongoing client contact. The plan will be prepared here by 'NEFA 501 practitioners,' many of whom are JDs [lawyers]. The fee for the plans will range between $500 and $5,000, based essentially on hours. The agent-marketer will get 15 percent of that fee for the delivery of the plan."

For those who want to have on-site presence but don't need the most elaborate of plans, NEFA has developed what it calls Edge I. This is an "entry level" plan. "In year one," says Brown, "the first $3,500 of the fee income will generate zero commission." The NEFA agent sends all fees to the home office, which in turn pays it out as a "commission." "Beyond $3,500, the agent gets 100 percent. We send them the 100 percent as a commission. In the second year of an ongoing practice, it pays a different schedule. The first $1,200 generates zero commission, $1,201 to $101,200 generates 90 percent commission. It [goes] from 90 percent to 92 percent to 95 percent to 98 percent."

The third and most complete option is to go full service with Edge II. For the first $7,500 in fees, the NEFA reps get zero commission, but they get 100 percent for anything over $7,501. In year two, they get zero commission up to $1,500 in fees and 100 percent of anything generated over that.

"We're deliberately eating money at the front end and expect to get it back down the road," Zilinski says. "The important principle is low entry. They have enough expenses up front. That accounts for why our business model says we needed 200 practices doing x amount by 1988 to keep the product effective. We are not anticipating turning the corner on profitability for those prices for nine years."

RESTRICTIONS OF JOINING A NATIONAL ORGANIZATION

To join the cozy "New England family," you need to be a career agent or a registered representative with New England Securities. "If you're not one or the other right now and you're not passing a certain amount of product through us, we don't offer the opportunity to join our family," Zilinski says in his Boston office, which overlooks part of Boston's fashionable Back Bay.

Obviously, while NEFA planners are fee-only and are not

required to sell only New England Securities Corporation products, The New England sees the opportunity for cross-selling and generating substantial commissions as a result of having the NEFA planning arm. But it also presents the same opportunity for the small agency that has both NEFA and New England Securities operations.

Bill Coulacos, a New England general agent who was part of the original joint venture and who runs Coulacos and Associates out of Toledo, Ohio, bears witness to the volume financial planning can generate through the equities arm of operations. While the financial planning services offered through NEFA are sold on a fee-only basis (because the home office perceives that prospective clients view that as a more objective arrangement), Coulacos has New England Securities at his disposal to implement the plans.

But even before NEFA existed, Coulacos was doing fee-based financial planning. Since 1982, he's served about ninety-four high-net-worth clients. His fees have ranged from $2,300 to $9,000. His clients' average net worth has been around $800,000; the average income $180,000. "With the higher net-worth client," Coulacos says, "we're not counting on selling them product. However, when we deliver the plan they virtually insist we implement. They don't just want to pay $3,000 to have a plan done." Of his ninety-four clients, all but two have implemented through Coulacos.

With the introduction of NEFA's Edge I plan, or miniplan, Coulacos sees even more opportunity for implementation of product. "There's a need for financial planning from the group of people whose incomes are $50,000 to $80,000 or $90,000, but they don't have the assets to pay a $2,300 fee. For $800 [for Edge I] we can take that individual and create a very helpful strategy. We look at being compensated for that market from the product being sold."

Coulacos thinks he'll have recouped any investment he's made into NEFA by the end of 1986. "We operate in the black every month now," he boasted. NEFA "will have a tremendous impact on product sales. . . . We anticipate commissions will amount to three times the fee we charge for plans."

Edge II, the more sophisticated of the financial plans NEFA can offer their higher net-worth clients, relies on Softbridge financial planning software, which is supplied to the

NEFA agent as part of his or her entry fee—another benefit that saves some money for the individual planner.

The smaller New England agencies recognize the advantages of hooking up with NEFA. Jerry Harvey, a New England general agent operating Harvey Financial Group in Austin, Texas, notes that "the sharing of ideas and developments has been better than sitting out here like a lonesome cowboy."

Individual financial planners can also take advantage of being covered by the national registered investment advisor (RIA) designation they will fall under by affiliating with NEFA. "We didn't have our own independent RIA," says David Plotkin. "One of the things NEFA has tried to do is keep up with the most stringent of regulations. Before I came here I looked at a good number of companies—private shops, insurance companies. I chose this route because here was this very conservative insurance company by nature, with lots of assets to back it up. Let's face it, they're in it [financial planning] to stay. They're not going to throw that much money down the tubes."

The national RIA umbrella and the strength of a company with $25 billion in assets under management are recurring strengths brought up by The New England agents who have bought into the NEFA network. But so is the ability to attract quality people to their operations—quality people like Plotkin—who are looking for a place to practice financial planning that will back them up with financial and marketing support.

"I think the number one point from my perspective," says Jerry Harvey, "is that NEFA is a tremendous tool for recruiting associates. The people we've brought in in the last couple of months are great. They can see that we're really doing financial planning. The quality people we're bringing in as a result of NEFA is really the biggest bang for our buck."

For some trying to set up their own shops, the timing of NEFA's national rollout has been superb. Stuart Migdon has been a public accountant for a number of years. Jim Figurelli, a New England general agent in Hackensack, New Jersey, was one of his clients. In April 1984, Figurelli hired Migdon to research and start up a financial planning operation. Asset Design Group kicked off in June 1985.

"We filed as an RIA at the end of 1984, hired a computer science student and an attorney, and kicked off," says Migdon. After Asset Design Group had done two plans, NEFA announced the national network. ADG signed up in September 1985.

"It gives me the experience of [The] New England. Their national marketing will help. My gut feeling is a very positive one. It'll be exciting to be in different publications. They've also researched the software and provided us with state-of-the-art software."

Bill Trull, an attorney, who in 1985 left Income and Capital Associates in Asheville, North Carolina (a firm affiliated with The New England), thinks NEFA is "trying to go first class. They appear to be putting in the financial resources to make it work."

He also thinks "they seem to be getting lost in their underwear to get the right type of software. They started out with ProPlan, then moved over to Softbridge . . . which has its drawbacks, too—like not being able to have integrated depreciation, which to me should be fairly standard in a high-class $4,000 or $5,000 package. Those enhancements are coming down the road."

In spite of his software views, Trull thinks NEFA will work. "[The] New England is a staid old company concerned about tarnishing their image. They're trying to spend the bucks to make sure they do it right."

THE AURA OF A
NATIONAL NETWORK

The New England has made painstaking efforts to get into the financial planning market carefully. Many of their NEFA planners will have the benefit of a built-in client referral network from the life insurance sales agent. NEFA planners can also enjoy the aura of being involved in a national network. While NEFA planners can retain their own identity, the national ad campaign will garner recognition for those who choose to bear the NEFA name and logo.

"It's an additional selling point," Zilinski says. "What financial planning clients wanted, particularly the corporate client, was to know who was standing behind the planner. Who stands behind the liability. Our people find it a major advantage to say they have a company with $25 billion in assets behind them."

While no The New England agent has turned down an offer to become a NEFA planner, there are still what Zilinski refers to as "nonbelievers." "I like to call them 'people who are waiting in the wings to see the results,' " Zilinski says. "They'll ultimately join it. When we first surveyed agents [in 1983], 20 percent said they needed it; 30 percent saw it as a possibility. Today, 50 percent see it as a need; 20 percent see it as a possibility. Since announcing [the national rollout in October 1985], we've been watching that 50 percent grow more and more. They're seeing that The New England is willing to stand behind it and watch the growth."

2 NAILING JELL-O TO THE WALL:
Spinning Off a Small Firm from a National Network

From time to time, any diligent observer will run across a good marketing story that involves innovation without controversy. Perhaps the story is about a new direct mail software package or a corporate design make-over. In any event, the situation will involve a likable wrinkle with little complication.

When Tom Hart gave a talk at the International Association for Financial Planning's (IAFP) Practice Management Conference held at the Bonaventure Hotel and Spa in Ft. Lauderdale, Florida, about how his financial planning firm, The First Continental Company, in Toledo, Ohio, gave its clients both a "value-perceived guarantee" and an "increase-your-net-worth-by-the-amount-of-our-fee-or-we'll-reimburse-the-difference-or-the-fee guarantee," it seemed to be just such a story.

Here was a financial planning firm that stood so solidly behind its work that it gave money-back guarantees. What's more, the firm had only once had a client ask for his money back based on the value-perceived guarantee. Hart was unfazed by that client's action, saying "We were happy to refund the money. Being that Toledo is such a small community, you don't want to have a guy unhappy."

Yet few things are as simple as they appear on the surface. Hart's marketing approach may seem straightforward, but as he notes, marketing is like "nailing Jell-O to the wall. Once you think you have it, it slips through your fingers." The marketing story of The First Continental Company shares that consistency.

ENTREPRENEURIAL ROOTS IN A NATIONAL FIRM

The real story of The First Continental Company begins with Tom Hart and Jeffrey Barefoot. These financial advisors had been running the financial planning shop for Coulacos and Associates, a Toledo-based The New England affiliate, when they made the transition to their own financial planning firm.

Bill Coulacos, a The New England general agent, had originally hired Jeffrey Barefoot, a CPA and JD, to run his financial planning operations just when The New England began its joint venture with general agents in the field, New England Financial Advisors, referred to as NEFA (see Chapter 1).

When Coulacos began his financial planning operation, it was clear to both him and Barefoot that it would be independent and fee-only. Coulacos's insurance agents could bring in clients, who would pay a fee for a financial plan. If the agents within the Coulacos and Associates insurance operation implemented the plans, they would get the commissions from the sale of products.

The plan at the outset was that Coulacos and Associates would operate as an independent registered investment advisor. Barefoot says that he agreed to work for a salary for two years from the time he started with Coulacos in October of 1983. For that salary he would create a text for the plan, pick software, hire staff, create a work flow, develop plans, and run all operations associated with the planning firm. In exchange for his sweat equity, Barefoot was to be a fifty-fifty partner with Coulacos once Coulacos had made back his initial, substantial investment in the start-up.

For the first couple of years, the planning operation meshed well with the firm. Coulacos and Associates—with the financial backing of Coulacos and the direction of Barefoot and newly hired fellow-CPA Tom Hart—had targeted the corporate market as its client base. The firm was successful at attracting executives from more than a half-dozen Fortune 500 companies that were located in the Toledo area.

The planners attracted their first Fortune 500 company executives by offering to do a pilot program with a few key executives to prove their expertise. "We're now doing ten or eleven of their top people," says Hart, "which might open up to another twenty middle-management people. Networking at the corporate level is phenomenal because a lot of these guys sit on each other's boards." So Barefoot and Hart found that their financial planning business was growing rapidly and that Coulacos and Associates was succeeding in this new venture.

Bill Coulacos was also one of the prime movers and innovators in the start-up of The New England's NEFA program. Ironically, the decision of a committee that Coulacos sat on ultimately caused Barefoot and Hart to venture out on their own.

Jim Zilinski, senior vice president of financial services marketing for The New England, explains that the split between the planners and the agency was "rooted predominantly in the direction we took when we decided to go with a national [registered] investment advisory. Bill Coulacos was the head of the general agents' committee that led us in that direction."

"We were stunned when Coulacos came back in September [1985] from Boston's meeting and said there were going to be some major changes," concurs Barefoot. "When we started a few years ago, we had an agreement that we would be grand-fathered in and would not have to join a national organization. When we began our marketing, we marketed to upscale clients as an independent organization."

Barefoot admits that The New England, unfortunately, never put this grandfather clause in writing. And while he felt Coulacos had done nothing wrong, neither did he want to give up the independence that Coulacos and Associates had always had.

"I don't blame him at all for what he had to do," says Barefoot. "In our community, I felt independence was more important. Not that New England doesn't have a good program, [but] we thought affiliating with NEFA would be the kiss of death to financial planning as we were doing it."

START-UP ISSUES

Barefoot gave notice in December 1985 and left Coulacos in mid-January. Hart followed suit and left at the end of February, having given Coulacos sixty days' notice. The pair promptly formed The First Continental Company, choosing that name, says Hart, because "we wanted a 'button-down' feel to it. When you think of First Continental, you might think of a bank."

Instead of using New England Securities Corporation, the planners now sell securities through Continental Capital Company, a Toledo broker-dealer that Hart and Barefoot also rent office space from. The relationship is a close one; Barefoot admits that the similarity between his firm's name and its broker-dealer's name is not all that coincidental.

Barefoot and Hart now also take commissions on product implementation. If clients ask them to implement the plans they prepare, their present arrangement differs from what they had with Coulacos and Associates. While the American Institute of Certified Public Accountants (AICPA) does not approve of CPAs taking commissions, Barefoot and Hart checked with the accountancy board of Ohio. The latter has no problem with commission-taking, and the pair fully disclose their compensation arrangement to clients.

Barefoot justifies receiving commissions on the grounds that they are used to offset the fee for the financial plan. He also says, however, that he doesn't agree with the AICPA's view on CPAs' taking commissions, so "I choose not to belong [to their organization] until they change that policy." (See Chapter 6.)

Like even the friendliest divorce, no separation is without its problems. In this case, one thorny issue is that of First Continental's luring away Coulacos's clients. Barefoot insists that he and Hart have only sent prospecting letters—announcing their new firm and requesting that the client sign for permission to have records transferred to First Continental—to those clients he and Hart personally brought in or those who requested to stay with Barefoot and Hart.

Coulacos has a different view: "All I know is that when he says that he only sent them to his own clients, that's not true. Some of my own clients got letters."

No one, including Hart and Barefoot, wants to think that First Continental "raided" the clients who might have been brought in by Coulacos's insurance agents. On the contrary, Barefoot insists that First Continental is only servicing these clients at their own request and that even then First Continental only takes a fee for its planning service; the Coulacos agent still gets all commissions for implementing the clients' plans.

Coulacos recognizes that since some clients had their plans begun by Hart and Barefoot, it is necessary for those clients to continue the relationship. But his policy is that new clients should not be referred to First Continental, since Coulacos and Associates continues to offer financial planning under the NEFA umbrella. "They [Coulacos's agents] can go to anybody they want to do business with, but they have to resign first," says Coulacos bluntly, when asked if he has any problem with his agents' bringing new clients over to First Continental.

Sidestepping the tricky question of whether Barefoot and Hart have diverted more clients from Coulacos than was strictly necessary, everyone involved in the breakup sings the praises of everyone else. Barefoot thinks Coulacos is a "visionary" for having been committed to financial planning so early on in the life of that industry.

At the home office of The New England in Boston, Zilinski remarks, "Barefoot is a damn good marketing guy. They're good guys, very aggressive, and we wish them the best." He adds, less charitably, "But we don't want them to walk out with clients that are perceived to be someone else's."

SPINNING OFF—
A NATURAL TURN

Was the move away from Coulacos an inevitable one? The two planners at First Continental say no. "I can honestly say that if [The] New England hadn't come in and told us we had to affiliate with them, we would have stayed with Bill [Coulacos]," admits Hart.

Zilinski observes that once the decision was made to form a national advisory under NEFA, all involved "saw the rules of the ball game change."

Zilinski makes it clear that New England never expected the program to be all of its agents' cup of tea. "About three or four out of every ten [agents] we approach don't immediately embrace NEFA," says Zilinski, "and the reasons may be the same as those Barefoot and Hart had to go out on their own. Any time you can hit six or seven, that's great. I would expect to see, of the forty-three [potential NEFA planners], three or four or five go different paths, while forty or so come on. If that were to happen, it would be an enormous retention rate.

"After five years, less than 25 percent of the people who enter the world as insurance agents are left. At New England, we range between 33 and 35 percent. If what I said occurred [with NEFA], we'd have a 75 to 80 percent retention rate."

The financial planning marketing ideas born at Bill Coulacos's operation were and will continue to be sound. They were sound enough that the pair took them over to First Continental. "The guarantees have had a lot to do with us getting business," says Hart. "I think the practice is going to become a necessity in the marketplace." Offering clients guarantees for services rendered is a sound way of demonstrating a willingness to stand behind your service. Such marketing will no doubt continue at both Coulacos's shop and First Continental.

It is also interesting to observe that very early on in the NEFA program, planners are beginning to spin off into their own independent operations—very much like CPAs leaving

Big Eight accounting firms to form their own shops (see Chapter 6). Ultimately, what Hart, Barefoot, and the other players involved in the start-up have learned is that even when the rules of the ball game change, there are plenty more fields on which to play ball.

3 A BANK WITHOUT WALLS:
Using Financial Planners for Market Research

Just as Jeffrey Barefoot and Thomas Hart recognized they could "play ball" by opening their own independent financial planning practice rather than continue with New England Financial Advisors, others in the financial services industry are recognizing that the rules are changing. To tackle big competition, innovation is necessary.

"Banks are beginning to realize they don't need bricks and mortar," observes Roger S. Walker, certified financial planner (CFP) and president of the Shorey-Huntington Corporation based in Concord, Massachusetts. In January 1986, when New England Federal Savings Bank became the first federally chartered savings bank in twenty-two years to open its doors in Massachusetts, its founders, Gerald Mueller and James Breznay, brought Walker's observation emphatically to life.

New England Federal will operate chiefly by mail, telephone, and both a regional and national automated teller machine (ATM) network. Jim Breznay, executive vice president, observes that although using mail and telemarketing may sound impersonal, many no-load mutual fund companies have proven just how successful you can be using these marketing techniques. Breznay thinks New England Federal can do even better than the mutual funds by assigning customers an account executive and giving them "the name of a person rather than just a number to call."

MARKET RESEARCH THROUGH A PROFESSIONAL NETWORK

When the founders of New England Federal wanted to tap a market that could lead them to a rich source of potential customers, they chose other financial services professionals. Financial planners were chief among these.

An integral aspect of the evolution of New England Federal was the input of the personal financial advisors with whom founders Gerald Mueller and James Breznay spent hours talking. The result, while not geared specifically to the needs of financial planning customers, promises to be a model bank, offering the kind of customer responsiveness that one associates with the financial planning profession.

Each customer of New England Federal will be assigned an account executive who will handle all of his or her questions, problems, and needs. Starting out, New England Federal had two account executives on staff. "We expect the number to grow as the number of customers grows," says Gerald Mueller, New England Federal's president. "They won't bounce you around from one person to another or switch you from extension to extension."

"The more the account executive understands the clients, the better off the clients are going to be," observes Roger Walker, a financial planner whose opinions Mueller and Breznay solicited when setting up shop. "That's true with what we as financial planners are doing with our clients as well."

Walker notes that many professions have lost the personalized approach. He points to the example of the health maintenance organization (HMO), which might save patients money but also, in most cases, requires that they see whatever doctor is available on a given visit. The person-to-person nature of the business is lost, Walker believes.

"Here's an opportunity to bring that back in banking," he says.

Breznay and Mueller raised $4 million through a public stock offering to start their bank. In the process of raising the capital, they also sought out the advice of professionals who could stimulate marketing ideas. "We think we can build a customer base faster if we gear toward the needs of particular industries," says Mueller. "Financial planners, lawyers, accountants—all have special needs."

This willingness to feel out financial planners for their ideas has made the new bank attractive to many planners in the field. "I think they're more willing to work with financial planners than other banks," says Earle Rugg, partner in Rugg and Tallman, an investment and tax planning firm in Worcester, Massachusetts.

Rugg's relationship to Mueller and Breznay goes back much further than the time they tapped him for advice. When the two founders were working at Freedom Federal Savings (which later merged into Northeast Savings Bank) in Worcester, Rugg was the bank's corporate counsel.

"Most banks want to do it all themselves," continues Rugg. "These people are willing to be creative in service, products, and marketing. We believe there is a tremendous marketplace out there of people who are confused by everything. We need to have credible people to rely on and have faith in. That can only be done through good service and product. . . . It's exciting to see a bank do something a little bit different."

In an environment in which financial planners are actively trying to carve out a niche for themselves in the marketplace of upscale clients, it is not surprising that a new bank would want to use planners as a resource for active market research.

"We talked to planners," says Mueller. "We wanted to see if we could provide products to appeal to them and their clients."

NEW PRODUCTS
AT A NEW BANK

Because New England Federal will have only one office, at its main location in Wellesley, and because there is not a lot of old debt, New England Federal's overhead is very low compared to that of most banks. Mueller and Breznay hope to pass their costs on to customers in the form of more attractive yields.

The main vehicles offered by New England Federal will not be all that different from a bank's standard fare—a variety of CDs, a money market deposit account, a money market checking account, and an IRA vehicle. They'll also offer a variety of real estate loans.

It is in the area of loan processing, however, that Mueller and Breznay think New England Federal can really be attractive to financial planners' customers. Financial planners "tell some real horror stories" says Mueller, about recommending a specific investment and having potential investors wait weeks for equity loans to be processed so they can have access to the cash to invest. "We want to make fast processing as high a priority as possible," adds Breznay.

For customers who want to tap some of the equity in their homes for a recommended investment, quick turnaround time is crucial. Mueller says New England Federal will be able to process equity loans in two days and first mortgage loans in seven days. "We can do it mainly because we've got decision-makers here and it won't be bouncing from one desk to another."

Bridge loans are another area where New England Federal

feels it might outperform the competition. Occasionally, there's a gap in the time it takes someone who has just closed on a new home to close on the house he or she just sold. To cover the purchase of the new home, which will utimately be covered by the old home's equity, a loan is often needed to bridge that gap. Roger Walker observes that some banks are reluctant to extend this type of loan even though the borrower is sitting on a tremendous amount of equity. Mueller understands the need for bridge loans. "It comes from treating people as being responsible adults who know what they're doing," he says.

IDENTIFYING
THE MARKET

The clientele that New England Federal is looking to attract are middle- to upper-middle-class clients who keep average balances of $25,000 to $30,000. Mueller and Breznay want active savers and investors who will be used to the ATM, bank by mail, and telemarketing approach that New England Federal is offering.

"What we're excluding is maybe 50 percent of the market that do nothing or very little with their money," says Mueller.

RAISING CAPITAL,
RAISING AWARENESS

Because they could not find a brokerage firm that would take them public, Mueller and Breznay raised the start-up funds themselves by selling $4 million in stock to nearly one hundred investors. Each of them owns 10,500 of those original shares, or 2.62 percent of the stock each.

"Going out and selling this ourselves has been extremely useful," says Mueller. "Mainly because we were getting out and talking with people and letting them know we wanted to do business. . . . At banks, officers don't generally deal with the customers."

In spite of their understanding of the marketplace, Mueller and Breznay realize that New England Federal will face some pretty heady competition in the banking industry. "Our competition is practically every financial institution that has had customers come to it," observes Mueller. But he and Breznay believe that their unique blend of offering high-tech, through the regional MONEC ATM network and the national PLUS ATM network, and high service, through personal account executives, will help them carve a solid niche for themselves.

They're also not too convinced that the large financial supermarkets pose a great threat to their new bank. "It's not all that clear that customers want the financial supermarket approach offered by a Sears or a Citibank," says Mueller. "The other approach is the niche or boutique approach. We figure that we're specialists, and if you want help in other areas, go to specialists in those areas."

For this reason, Mueller and Breznay are building a list of referrals in financial service areas outside of banking. They hope that professionals, including financial planners, will reciprocate. But they're not relying solely on referrals to build a customer base. To get a faster start, they've opted to advertise aggressively in the Boston newspapers.

"Banks are just now becoming a little marketing oriented," says Mueller. "For too long we just threw open our doors and said, 'Here are our rates. Take it or leave it.' Deregulation has made it much more competitive."

While Mueller and Breznay may have begun their calls on outside professionals to find potential investors, the end result was guidance on how to tailor their bank's services and products to the needs of those financial services customers. In the process, they've managed to build a referral network that just might draw customers into the bank when they need outside financial advice.

While being the new kid on the banking block might make New England Federal's officials more aggressive in the marketplace, one of the nagging doubts that Breznay and Mueller have to be facing is whether or not they can lure customers away from their big-name competitors.

In spite of the vocal support from financial planners in the field, Mueller admits, "Bank of Boston's probably not going to feel us for some time to come."

4 THE CHAIN GAIN:
Developing a New Product Concept— Business Partnerships

In March 1987, Ken Peterson, chairman of the Financial Equity Group (FEG), Inc., a publicly held developer of public and private investment programs based in Birmingham, Michigan, stood at the podium in a conference room of the McClean (Virginia) Hilton Hotel. Since 1968, Peterson had worked in financial planning, oil and gas partnership development, private equipment leasing partnership development, and a variety of real estate deals.

But now he faced what might be his toughest audience—a group of registered representatives from broker-dealers he was trying to sell on the idea of business partnerships, or more specifically, a private placement investing in a chain of specialty sporting-goods stores.

RECOGNIZING A
PRODUCT OPPORTUNITY

Merle Harmon's Fan Fair is a chain of specialty sporting-goods stores that began in 1977 in Milwaukee to sell licensed goods from the NFL, NBA, and other professional sports groups.

Merle Harmon had been the broadcaster for the Milwaukee Brewers and Braves baseball teams and is now an announcer for the Texas Rangers home games on cable television. By the end of 1986, Harmon had expanded his chain to more than seventy stores. A minority were company owned; the majority were owned by franchisees. Peterson and FEG were the ticket Harmon needed to bring a capital infusion and massive expansion to his already successful Fan Fair Development Corporation, based in New Berlin, Wisconsin.

FEG bought the exclusive franchise rights to Fan Fair from Virginia to Maine on the East Coast and in all of California except for Los Angeles and Orange County. By packaging groups of stores together in private placement offerings, FEG was to act as general partner and sell off units to limited partners. By 1991, they hoped to develop ninety-five stores on the East Coast and another forty to fifty stores on the West Coast, according to Peterson.

SELLING THE OFFBEAT: TEACHING THE RETAIL TRADE

But before he sold anything, Peterson had to convince this group sitting before him why investing in something as seemingly offbeat as a private placement of specialty sports stores made sense.

"Most of you have accumulated a wealth of knowledge over your careers in real estate, in oil and gas and equipment leasing, and other special situations," Peterson told the crowd, "but many of you have not had an opportunity to look at a business venture as a viable opportunity for either partnership or otherwise. . . . So we thought it would be important to try to create a forum to provide you with the background information that we think is essential to the credibility of this type of offering."

What followed was four hours of lessons in retailing—specialty and otherwise. Experts on franchise site selection, retailing consultants, and a marketing expert armed with demographics held forth explaining the ins and outs, risks and rewards, potentials and pitfalls of the retailing trade.

Merle Harmon himself gave the crowd a spiritual pep talk: "Financial Equity is bringing the capital in. . . . We're the vehicle; Financial Equity is supplying something we need; so as partners we come together [lifts hands, intertwines fingers]. We came together and we can be successful together."

Frank Vuono, director of licensing and development for NFL Properties (the guys who say what's okay and what's not okay to do with NFL logo items) gave the group the stats they wanted to hear: "Merle Harmon's Fan Fair has the most stores and is the most prominent licensed fan store in the country. The next closest competitor maybe has thirty locations. . . . You're really looking at the preeminent licensed fan store."

Yes, but is there a market for the stuff these stores are selling?

"Last year," Vuono told the crowd, "the retail market was $257 billion . . . licensing itself as an overall business represented 20 percent of that (a $50.7 billion market). Twenty-eight billion dollars is in sporting goods, and 28 percent of the sporting goods market is in licensed products. . . . It's a $7.8 billion market, and it's not even been scratched. . . . Our business over the past three years has been up over 35 percent a year, and that's on record volumes."

What's fueled the growth?

"The baby boomers have grown up. The Sears kids [who once wore NFL pajamas] are now wearing adult apparel. . . . But the biggest reason is television. Every time an NFL football game is on the tube it's a three-hour advertisement for our product. . . . As long as there's sports shown on TV every day, as long as there's sports written about every day, there'll be a business. How much it will grow, we don't know, but it's not reached . . . saturation yet. . . . There will be some fallout, but a company like Merle Harmon's will benefit from the fallout."

Gary Hurvitz, president of H. Beck, Inc., a broker-dealer in Silver Springs, Maryland, hears Vuono's message loud and clear. "I don't know if you were watching 'The Today Show' this morning," he says later, referring to a morning the show was on location in Minnesota. "Bryant Gumbel and Jane Pauley got up and put on their Minnesota Twins jackets." Sale of Twins jackets in Fan Fair stores soar in Hurwitz's mind. "Something like 48 percent of [all homes] in America has at least one NFL-licensed product," he gleams.

SELLING THE TRACK
RECORD OF FRANCHISING

The hardest thing about selling the concept of a franchise retail specialty store, Peterson would say, long after the McClean meeting had made its converts, was "trying to give the broker-dealer, and ultimately the investor, an understanding of what franchising is and what retailing is. First of all, let's look at franchising and its track record put out by the Department of Labor—95 percent of all franchisers succeeded at the end of sixty months and 90 percent after ten years as opposed to nonfranchises, which only succeed at the rate of 18 percent after ten years."

Peterson's figures may seem optimistic when compared to *Inc.* magazine's recent report that a record 78 franchises failed in 1986, which resulted in leaving 5,667 franchise units stranded. There's the key; it's not the number of franchises that fail, but the number of units those franchises leave in their trail.

Venture magazine's most recent "Franchisor 100" survey

reported that more than 2,000 business-format franchises, a category that Merle Harmon's Fan Fair falls squarely into, exist in the United States today. The total number of units run by these companies is more than 300,000. But in spite of the growing number of failures, more and more franchise upstarts enter into the fray. The growth is astounding, perhaps fueled by a burgeoning service economy or the vast expanse of malls existing and going up around the country, which guarantee store operators more predictable market traffic. Stan Luxenberg, in his book *Roadside Empires: How the Chains Franchised America* (Viking, 1985), reports that the sales of business-format franchises nearly doubled from 1978 to 1983.

Peterson is quick to point to Fan Fair's track record of success. "We have to say that this is not a venture capital deal. Merle Harmon's Fan Fair has been in business for ten years and never closed a store. In the event that we had one or two that didn't do well, we would move it. To relocate it would cost $40,000 or $50,000, which is not very prohibitive."

LEAPING INTO
A NEW AREA

"Everyone considers retailing a much higher risk because there's not an underlying asset," says Hurvitz of H. Beck, Inc. "But somewhat ameliorating that in this case is that it's a national chain of eighty-five [sic] stores, so there is a track record of the chain itself, which relieves some of the comparative anxiety. We were not in the market for retailing opportunities, but on the other hand when one comes across like this, we spent four months kicking the tires.... It's a chance to participate at a relatively early stage in a potentially growing industry. The potential returns are substantial compared to the risk involved.... There's sex appeal, but besides sex appeal, here is a retailing business that is growing at a rate of 35 percent a year."

"It was a real leap into a new area for us," says Charles Nance, staff lawyer and due diligence director for Derand Investment Corporation, a broker-dealer based in Arlington, Virginia.

REVENUE ASSUMPTIONS

Peterson assumes "that the first-year revenue in these [Fan Fair] stores [in the partnership] will equal $250,000, and that there will be a 6 percent increase in sales thereafter.... We have found, for example, in an existing metropolitan store, average sales were in excess of $450,000. As of December of 1985, the average Fan Fair store that had been in business for two years or longer did $353,000 in sales. The year before that it did $281,000 in sales. So we're basically using numbers that we believe are 15 to 20 percent below current national averages in the same business."

OPENING CLIENTS' MINDS TO NEW CONCEPTS

"Clients have the same problem I did in deciding to look into a new area," says Nance. "Some are just turned off; some very excited, because they are just surrounded by sports all the time.... Our willingness to look at Fan Fair has made us more willing to look into other business partnerships.

"One of the nice things [about it] is that if you buy a piece of real estate and it's not doing well, you can't move it; with a franchise, you're not wedded to one location forever. It gives you a different orientation where you can pick up and move if you have to.

"It's very different from what people have been selling. To the extent that people didn't want to hear about partnerships at the end of 1986, this one is different enough that it captured their imagination."

Nance likens Fan Fair and other business partnerships to investments in cable limited partnerships, which his firm has packaged private placements in for some time. "Early on, cable was stuck back in a corner [at conventions of investment offerings]. Now cable is mainstream. I think retail will be the same. We're actually doing an additional partnership of fast food franchises in California."

FACING THE ECONOMIC CLIMATE

But beyond selling his broker-dealers on the specialty retailing franchised store concept, Peterson faced a climate where investors were not showering a great deal of favor on private placement deals.

"One of the reasons [private placements] have not been as popular," he says, "is that traditionally they've focused on providing two things: shelter for investors and high compensation for brokers. In effect, [the] tax reform [of 1986] has resulted in a volume of these [tax shelters] disappearing.

"Quite frankly, [these partnerships] are designed to throw off the maximum return on investment. We've tried to design the package to stand on its own and provide good economics and a realistic return to investors. It isn't necessarily going to solve anybody's problem if they were involved in passive income in the past. It's basically a conservative, economic investment with fairly sound projections if everything goes according to plan."

"It's an operating business, which is a different breed from most private placements," says one senior analyst with a New England broker-dealer selling Fan Fair units. "There's no shelter of the tax flow. The name of the game is cash, cash, cash. There's no tax shelter whatever."

Peterson and FEG have also tried to temper the impact a high broker-dealer commission can have on an investor's private placement dollars. "We pay a standard 10 percent compensation to a broker-dealer," Peterson says. "If a broker-dealer takes down a whole deal with us, then we pay them an extra 2 percent. . . . With a total load of 15 percent, that makes it a relatively small amount of funds which are being taken off to cover for offering expenses by comparison with some other programs which could run 20 or 25 or 28 percent."

"Basically our feeling is one that it's an appropriate post-TRA 86 [Tax Reform Act of 1986] investment," says Hurvitz. "There is some unsheltered passive income over a period of time, but we're not directing it just at people who want to offset passive losses, but at people who want to make money. The interest in the product is not for a tax shelter or really as a passive income generator (PIG). It really is for its investment potential. This thing can make money, whether it's shelter, passive, active. This thing can make money, and that's what people are looking for and probably should have been looking for.

"When I talk about making money—this definitely can make real money. As it makes money and expands, that back-end value goes up. It's similar to raising rents in a building. Here you're looking at nice income. Unlike leveraged real estate where depreciation can be substantial, this is designed to just make money."

THE "IN OUR OWN BACKYARD" PHENOMENON

Another problem Peterson says he faced, beyond the new concept and private placement issue, was the "in our own backyard" phenomenon.

"Broker-dealers in Richmond have consistently said to us that they only like private placements developed in their own region," says Peterson, so they can drive up the street, have lunch, and look at the store. We've run into it . . . a parochial view of, 'We like to put our money in our backyard; our investors want to see things in their own backyard.' I don't think most investors care, quite frankly, they just are interested in the economics, but a lot of broker-dealers have that mentality that investors don't want to see an investment if it's not in their own backyard.

"So much of the sales is in the salesman. The investor is looking to the broker-dealer, registered representative, or financial planner and their analysis on that situation rather than other issues of whether or not he can drive over and look at the store."

THE PRODUCT'S SPECIFICS

FEG has so far put together seven private placements, ranging in size from twenty-eight units at $26,000 a unit ($728,000 total) to seventy-three units at $31,000 a unit ($2.263 million total). The first two offerings, Washington, DC Fan Fair Partners I and New England Fan Fair Partners I, closed in early 1987. Both raised $728,000. Both invested in a blind pool (no specific listings) of locations within the respective regions. All subsequent offerings (New England II, Washington II, Coastal States, Virginia I, and San Francisco I) specified store locations by mall site with the right of substitution.

Peterson, as general partner, receives a one-time $15,000 partnership fee for getting each program organized, an $18,000 per-store fee to cover site location and development work (up from $15,000 per store in New England I and Washington I; if a store is moved, there is no additional site fee), $1,000 per month as an investor services fee, and an annual management fee equal to 5 percent of gross revenues.

The franchisor (Merle Harmon's organization) receives a franchise fee of $15,000 per store from partnership equity and 4 percent of gross revenues per year as a royalty fee.

JUSTIFYING
MANAGEMENT COSTS

"I somewhat question FEG's extra finder's fee cost," says the senior analyst with the New England broker-dealer. "You have to look at the unaffiliated franchisee's costs and the cost of buying through FEG, and that's the only markup I see. The benefits are diversity within the partnership. I don't see a lot of downside to the product because they're not going to be foreclosed on, which can do hell to a limited partner's account."

Peterson explains the extra cost. "We've negotiated area exclusivity from Fan Fair, which allows the stores to pick up some economies. There are discounts on the fees we pay to Fan Fair. The normal franchise fee is $20,000; we pay $15,000. Most owners would pay a 5 percent royalty on gross sales; we pay a 4 percent royalty. And we pass those discounts on.

"We're compensated because our management company [Franchise Management Corporation] is paid an $18,000 per-site fee, which is compensation for the site selection process, a feasibility study of the market area, the lease negotiation with the mall, negotiations with contractors, and basically coordinating all the preopening activities.

"Quite frankly," a phrase Peterson, quite frankly, uses quite often, "an individual franchisee would have to pay someone to do this anyway."

"There *are* substantial fees," says Hurvitz, "but when you are dealing with retailing as opposed to an office building, it's a very management-intensive business. In a management-intensive business, you want management to be well rewarded. It's not one of these deals where you can look at it and say the general partner is making too much. The general partner is really responsible not just for structuring [the deal] but making it work."

"The interesting thing," says Peterson, "is that most of the people that contact franchisors in the United States really don't have the resources to do even one store or more. . . . What we're doing, at the risk of suggesting this is a public service, is that we're really providing a lot of opportunities for investors who may not have $100 or $200 or $500 million to participate in a business format without worrying about showing up at the store on a Saturday if someone calls in sick, without that hands-on responsibility, and yet they can participate with relatively little dilution. . . . That's one of the reasons why direct participation products in businesses are going to grow in the next several years."

An Escape Clause for Investors

One of the most attractive features of the partnerships that plays on Peterson's public service persona is a "right of presentment," an escape clause with a nine-year window of opportunity for the wary investor to get out of the deal. "There's a method for taking out an individual investor who may want to liquidate their interest prior to termination of the partnership, whenever that would be," says Peterson.

"And that is on a formula basis essentially to provide them with a safety net price, if you will. It's a minimum purchase, which is calculated on the basis of four times the cash flow from the store's operation computed over the last four quarters prior to their submission of their interest. It's a very simple calculation.

"Essentially we take the aggregate cash flow of the fifteen stores. In this case let's pick a number and say it's a million dollars. We don't take anything off for tax consequences. We don't take anything off for depreciation, so it's a high number. If there is some debt associated with the management of the stores, then we would also subtract that debt. It would probably be modest, if any, because no debt is projected. . . . Take that $1 million, multiply by four, and you have a $4 million asset, divide it by the number of units [in the partnership], and that would be the purchase price that the investor would be entitled to.

"The terms of the buyout are a leveraged buyout, meaning that we will give them 25 percent down and the balance of their 75 percent value over a thirty-six month-period, plus interest at 2 [percent] over [the] prime [lending rate] floating, so they'd have a cash flow stream."

But Peterson would be hard-pressed to explain or predict why anyone would want out. The first partnership store was opened in November 1986. Other openings followed. By March 1987, nine stores were in operation. Collectively, Peterson told the McClean group, the stores had $480,000 in sales and would hit the $500,000 mark by the end of March 1987.

"So we're now more of a believer than when we were doing our due diligence in this effort," he says.

TAKING THE PRIVATE
CONCEPT PUBLIC?

What's next on Peterson's list of challenging sells in the investment world? Well, he'd really like to do a public business partnership offering.

"The public fund is a better vehicle because you get a true blind pool and can cherry-pick and get the best locations. If you're doing a series of private placements, because of the thirty-five-investor limitation, you run into a securities integration problem if you do a blind pool." [This is one of the reasons why, after the first two Fan Fair private placements, the offerings specified mall locations.] "It creates a much higher challenge, because you notify the malls but you may not want to sign a lease for three or four months [until the deal is put together].

"I think the attractiveness from a public point of view is that there are not significant additional costs for syndication or acquisitions. . . . Because of the type of partnership this is, we can buy a number of sites for a relatively low cost. We now spend $122,000 per site to get the store up and running. Our legal fees in a large [private] partnership would be $20,000 for a $1 million offering; probably $60,000 or $70,000 for a large public fund—a $15 to $20 million fund. Two significant advantages would be that we would not be restricted to any area except from a management standpoint. The second is that we would be able to include more than one [type of] business. The ability to participate in, say, five to ten business entities would give us even more diversification.

"The only thing wrong with the public program is you're going to have to consistently compete with private placements. A broker-dealer can make more [in a private placement offering], since any public deal has a 10 percent commission limitation plus .5 percent for due diligence.

"But the only thing holding us back on a public fund is that our costs of getting up and marketed would be at least $400,000. If I had an unlimited expense account, there's no question I'd have that product on the street. Someone's going to do it; it's inevitable. I think we could put together a team that's unrivaled."

Beyond the public offering is a dream that has intrigued Peterson for the last ten to twelve years, a dream that prior to now would probably have been his most difficult sell ever. In light of the fact that professional basketball's Denver Nuggets and Boston Celtics have gone public with stock offerings in one form or another, Peterson's dream of syndicating an NFL football team just might materialize one of these days in an offering on a broker-dealer's desk.

PART TWO
PRODUCT OR SERVICE DIFFERENTIATION

Product or service differentiation entails making your product or service more appealing or better in some way than your competitor's, to appeal to the same overall market.

While the concept may sound simple, too often the execution is not. Frequently, financial services professionals pay little heed to making themselves attractive to their marketplace, but rather follow the herd of professionals who have set up shop before them with the same marketing strategies.

To give your product or service the appearance of being better than the one being sold by the financial professional down the block, you need to differentiate yourself from the crowd.

Bob Levoy, a consultant out of Great Neck, New York, has been advising professionals for years to find their differential competitive advantage and market it to their prospective customers. In Chapter 5, Levoy shares his insight into how professionals can set themselves apart from the crowd without stooping to what he refers to as "tacky" marketing practices.

With the need for financial planning services growing among consumers, it was only a matter of time before one of their most trusted financial advisors—the accountant—sought to add financial planning services to their menu of offerings. By 1986, CPAs accounted for 13 percent of the membership of the International Association for Financial Planning (IAFP). When the American Institute of Certified Public Accountants (AICPA) announced the formation of a financial planning division in the summer of 1986, 5,000 CPAs signed up. The desire to differentiate themselves by offering more than just the usual accounting services led two former CPAs in 1985 to form the American Association of Personal Financial Planners (AAPFP), a for-profit service organization exclusively for CPAs. Chapter 6 looks at the transition many CPAs are making to the CPA–financial planner role. It looks at how these CPAs must understand a new market, deal with industry regulatory issues, and establish a new network of professionals after they have assumed their new role.

Softbridge Microsystems Corporation, a software firm based in Cambridge, Massachusetts, seeks to differentiate itself from the crowd of financial planning software companies by offering what its management refers to as "relationship marketing"—an aggressive campaign to be responsive to customer needs and desires in their product. Chapter 7 looks at the success Softbridge has been having with this technique and at the success the financial professionals who use its software are having using the same principle of relationship marketing. Being responsive to customer requests and needs is differentiating these professionals from the "love them and leave them crowd," which simply provides a product or service and is infrequently heard from again.

5 THE COMPETITIVE ADVANTAGE

The Sheraton-Mansfield Hotel lies in a secluded wooded area in northeast Massachusetts. Robert Levoy, director of Professional Practice Consultants in Great Neck, New York, will be conducting a seminar here.

Since 1968, Levoy has conducted more than 2,500 seminars for professionals in a wide variety of fields, ranging from optometry and dentistry to accounting and financial planning. Financial planning is the newest of the professions on his list of seminar clients. Levoy added it about three years ago when he was asked to conduct a seminar for a national meeting of the International Association for Financial Planning (IAFP) in Boston.

The television set is on in Harry's, one of the Sheraton's lounges. The first round of "Jeopardy" is on, and Alex Trebek has pointed out that no one has yet to call any of the cards in the Indian sayings category. Sure enough, the contestant from New Jersey calls the category for $20 on his next turn.

The answer is "a ceremonial feast of the Chinook Indians to validate tribal position, accompanied by a lavish distribution of gifts."

The silence deafens. Two guys watching television from the bar mull it over. They don't know the answer either. The bartender finishes drying a highball glass, puts it on the rack, looks up at the TV set, and says "Potlach," just as the buzzer goes off.

Trebeck tells the three contestants and the audience at home, "The correct answer is, 'What is potlach?' " The two guys at the bar order another round.

Levoy has arrived and checked in. He's a tall man, dressed conservatively in a gray herringbone jacket, black slacks, a red and black rep tie, a white Oxford cloth shirt, and black shoes.

In most established professions, there are seminars available to instruct the professional in almost all aspects of his or her business. Marketing is certainly one of those aspects. If being lumped in with other established professions is any indication of a maturing industry, financial planning has arrived. There are dozens of individuals and companies that will put on a seminar to tell you what you need to do to capture your market. Some will put on the seminars in order to sell a wide variety of books, videotapes, and other source material. Others will try to capture some individual consulting business.

Levoy doesn't fall into either of these categories. He

charges a flat fee for his seminars, which varies depending on the length of the seminar. For a recent morning presentation to financial planners, he was compensated with $2,000 for his time. For a day-long address to dentists, he got $3,500. He doesn't do any individual consulting. He doesn't peddle his books when he runs a seminar. Levoy thinks that's part of what he calls "tacky marketing," a phenomenon of gimmicky come-ons and sales pitches that he'd like to erase from the marketing of all professional practices.

THE THREE-STRATEGY APPROACH TO CAPTURING A MARKET

Levoy's marketing pitch to financial planners is simple. He basically calls for a three-strategy approach to attracting the potential market:

1. Find a differential competitive advantage.
2. Understand and identify client needs.
3. Know your own strengths and weaknesses.

At his seminars, Levoy will help the audience members grapple with each of these strategies. At a recent seminar for financial planners, for instance, he held up a tape-recorded statement of philosophy that one planner had sent to his prospective clients.

"How many of you are doing this?" Levoy asked his audience. One or two out of a room of a hundred-plus planners raised their hands.

Here was a differential competitive advantage one planner had found. "I like it because no one else is doing it," Levoy told his audience.

THE THREE Rs: RAPPORT, REPUTATION, REFERRALS

In addition to the three strategies, Levoy emphasizes the need to develop what he calls the three Rs: rapport, reputation, and referrals. Again, obvious links to successfully marketing a practice.

"It *is* obvious," Levoy says. "People come and hear me and say it's common sense but that they needed to hear it."

Marcia Wimmer, a certified financial planner (CFP) with Interwest Financial Advisors in Portland, Oregon, who has attended two Levoy marketing seminars, concurs. "Even though it may be obvious, it helps to have him point it out," says Wimmer. "Especially the stories of successful planners he incorporates into his presentation. It's helpful to know what makes someone else successful and to know what we're doing might be the same as the people we admire."

Levoy will insist, however, that his seminars are not intended to be motivational. "If it gets people juiced up, it's an afterthought. To me, all motivation is self-motivation. What I'm trying to do is light fires inside of them."

He's lighted fires inside Charles Lefkowitz, CFP with Financial Blueprints, Inc., in Florham Park, New Jersey, who has attended many Levoy seminars. "Every time I hear him I enjoy him and get an idea or two out of him," Lefkowitz says. "In an early seminar, I remember him talking about going that one step extra, that little bit of extra service that makes you different. It's really a combination of his reaffirming what I'm already doing as well as forcing me to pay more attention to things I might not be doing."

For all intents and purposes, Levoy *does* motivate his audiences, with a blend of humor and practical marketing advice. Peppered throughout his talks are sayings he attributes to his grandmother.

"As my grandmother used to say," he'll say at a lull in the presentation, "when you lose confidence in yourself, you make it unanimous."

Or, "As my grandmother used to say, the size of your funeral (pause) depends upon the weather."

He draws laughs. He keeps his audience awake. He also has some set ideas of what's marketing and what's not.

DEFINING MARKETING

Levoy distinguishes marketing from advertising and promotional efforts.

Most marketing professionals will concede that advertising and promotions are part of the overall process of marketing, but at his seminars, Levoy vehemently draws a distinction, choosing to define marketing as the three-strategy approach mentioned earlier. At the seminars he often mentions what he perceives to be the five biggest problems with advertising and promotions:

1. It's too expensive.
2. You have to work fast to be able to handle the high volume advertising will generate.
3. There's a great pressure to close sales.
4. The relationship with the client could become tenuous.
5. And if you discount fees as a come-on, a lot of people may associate low fees with low quality.

Levoy might wrap up by asking his audience, "Did you ever have the feeling that the light at the end of the tunnel was the headlights of an oncoming train?"

"The average professional person is not like the average businessperson," Levoy says. "There's a certain commitment to client service. There's a love, a passion for whatever it is they're doing. The more involved with promotion and advertising a person is, the more removed he becomes from the hands-on portion of his profession."

A PASSION FOR THE
HANDS-ON

It's his own background that reaffirmed Levoy's notion that the true professional should, as Tom Peters and Richard Waterman, Jr., wrote in *In Search of Excellence*, "stick close to the knitting."

Levoy, who is a licensed optometrist but chose not to practice, started running seminars part-time toward the end of his career in marketing and management with Christian Dior in the mid-1960s. He began running seminars full-time in 1968. But the seminars of twenty years ago differed from the solo seminars he runs today.

"In the beginning, I'd package programs and put together a coterie of speakers," Levoy says. "I would select the speakers and do a direct mail campaign to attract potential attendees. Each profession had its own program. They were upscale programs. The best speakers. Nicest hotels. Super meals. We never did spectacularly well financially, because everything was first class. We wouldn't cut corners. We spoiled everybody. They really got their money's worth and then some.

"But probably 60 to 65 percent of my job ended up being administrative, which meant that I spent 60 to 65 percent of my time doing something I really didn't want to do."

So Levoy shifted his approach to seminars and began running one-man presentations, which gave him more of the "hands-on" he wanted.

Underlying his marketing seminar theme is the message to avoid advertising and promotions because they just might remove you from what you wanted to do in the first place.

Instead, he says, look for the differential competitive advantage, which in many cases comes down to keeping up with the times and trends. "The old formulas don't work anymore," Levoy tells his audiences. "Ask Coca Cola."

MARKET RESEARCH AND THE COMPETITIVE ADVANTAGE

Levoy tries to practice what he preaches. He considers his own differential competitive advantage to be that his seminars are grounded in market research, which he admits is flavored by his own experiences and insights.

Levoy's market research is gathered from practitioners, clients, and office personnel. He'll do interviews, telephone surveys, and questionnaires to gather information about the various professions. His brand of market research is not one that boasts databases and elaborate extrapolations but one more in keeping with the practical, hands-on nature of his seminar presentations.

Marcia Wimmer thinks Levoy's market research pays off in his seminar presentations. "At both sessions I attended, he arrived early and ready to work. He met with planners to try to get a better idea of what our business was all about. Because he worked hard to learn more about our business, the points he made were based on the realities of the financial planning industry. It made it real life. The result was that he wasn't only entertaining, but educational as well."

"I was called by MIT to do a program," Levoy tells me.

"Two one-day programs for administrative supervisors and personnel on the subject of team-building and employee motivation. I asked, 'You've got the Sloan School of Management right there, why are you calling me to come up there?' The answer was, 'You're practical.' I consider that the absolute compliment of my career. That's what I'm really trying to be. That's what it's all about."

Bob Levoy likes to joke with his audiences that if he had all the answers in marketing, he'd retire to the island of Eleuthra in the Bahamas. In fact, there's a private club renowned for its incredible service in Eleuthra's Governor's Harbor called Potlach. In his book, *The Successful Professional Practice* (Prentice-Hall, 1970), which remains in print despite the fact that Levoy wrote it more than fifteen years ago, Levoy tells of his stay at Potlach. He writes:

> I was curious about the name "Potlach" and discovered it is derived from an Indian expression meaning. "I give you more than you give me." This philosophy encompasses a world of practice building. It is the distilled concept of humanizing professional relations. It is a fountainhead of good will.

Levoy and the bartender at the Sheraton-Mansfield may be among the small cadre of people who know the true meaning of *potlach*. But Levoy would have us believe that its essence is what lies at the heart of every truly successful professional.

6 FINDING THE EDGE:
CPAs Shift to Financial Planning

"There's no question that a growing number of certified public accountants [CPAs] are at least looking at financial planning," says Mark Bass from the Lubbock, Texas, office of Pennington/ Bass Companies. Bass is a certified financial planner (CFP) who earned his CPA designation to understand "how his accounting clients think." He has never practiced public accounting.

Certified public accountants have been eyeing the financial planning market for years. In 1986 alone, CPAs accounted for 13 percent of the membership of the International Association for Financial Planning (IAFP). And while some of these CPAs may not be practicing accounting publicly, many are.

"Part of the problem with the accountants is that they think they do financial planning anyway," says Diane Lapon, CFP with Seidman Financial Services in Boston. "You have to get them to realize the difference between what they are already doing and financial planning."

REPOSITIONING TO A READY-MADE CLIENT BASE

As CPAs reposition themselves for serving up comprehensive financial planning to their clientele, they face difficult issues.

"They have a ready-made client base and are doing some aspects of financial planning already," says Bass, who quickly adds, "although in nearly every case, they are not doing as much financial planning as they think they are. Financial objectives and [the client's] temperament are two major areas in which they have to get knowledge."

"There's clearly a growing trend," says Jerry Cohen, president and cofounder of the American Association of Personal Financial Planners (AAPFP), a for-profit service organization he founded in 1985 with fellow CPA Roy Weitz, to "serve the professional needs of the CPA-financial planner." The AAPFP, which now has approximately 250 members, who each pay an annual membership fee of $195, requires only that its members be CPAs.

"That the AICPA [American Institute of Certified Public Accountants] had several thousand CPAs—in the area of 5,000—join up in its personal financial planning division when it was formed in the summer of 1986 is a good indication of interest," says Cohen. "Over the two years we've been involved, we have definitely seen a growing interest. Over the years, more CPAs will look to get involved."

The match between the CPA and the financial planning profession is to many a natural one. "We think it's good because they have such a strong relationship with the clients," observes Cohen. "They already have the confidence of clients and some knowledge; the next step is to take it further and do comprehensive financial planning. Some have been doing a piece of it, but never comprehensive financial planning."

UNDERSTANDING THE
NEW MARKET

"The biggest mistake that CPAs will make coming into this market is that they will approach it as something for their tax planning department to do the other six months of the year," says Larry W. Carroll, CFP, who runs Carroll Financial Planning Associates, Inc., in Charlotte, North Carolina.

Carroll, himself a CPA who no longer practices publicly, continues: "The only way for the CPA to be successful in financial planning is to set up a financial planning department with full-time people and hardware and software and someone to be accountable for success. Most of them are not inclined to make that commitment. Planning is a full-time business. When the client has questions, he doesn't want to have to wait when he needs his questions answered."

THE REGULATORY
HURDLES

Beyond the problem of identifying the difference between tax planning and financial planning, CPAs entering the financial planning marketplace have to wrestle with the sticky issue of regulation. First off, there is the decision about whether or not to register as an investment advisor with the Securities and Exchange Commission (SEC).

"The big dilemma for accountants," observes Christiane Delessert, Seidman Financial Services' national technical director, "is what do you do with investment advice? We take the position that even [if you are giving] general investment advice, you have to be registered."

Larry Carroll agrees. "There's no doubt in my mind that the CPA should be registered if he is functioning in the role planners must assume if they are going to be successful. General advice won't suffice. The client wants to know answers. A good planner has to go to the point of giving specific advice and be accountable for his advice."

And then the CPA has to wrestle with whether or not to be fee-only or to accept commissions on products. If they follow the Code of Ethics of the American Institute of Certified Public Accountants (AICPA), their professional organization, there is little doubt that they should not be accepting commissions for sale of any products.

But like everything in finances and regulation, the issue is not that simple.

While the AICPA makes commission-taking a taboo, not all state accountancy boards are in agreement. The Texas State Board of Public Accountancy revised its Rules of Professional Conduct, effective November 17, 1986, eliminating its ban on accepting commissions. Obviously this runs counter to the AICPA Code of Ethics.

Other state boards think differently from Texas. The California Society of Certified Public Accountants, in its January 1987 *Monthly Statement*, "strongly opposes accepting commissions," going so far as to say, "Entering into such arrangements could result in loss of certificate and/or membership."

Even the players themselves have differing views. Says Delessert, whose Seidman Financial Services is an offshoot of the large accounting firm Seidman and Seidman/BDO: "We do not sell; no commissions. We see it as a terrible conflict."

Larry Carroll believes it's okay to accept commissions, but only when and if the AICPA changes its Code of Ethics, and even then he has problems with practicing public accountants taking commissions. "I really don't have a problem with a CPA taking commissions if it's on a fully disclosed basis and if his Code of Ethics provides for it, then it's fine. But it's probably not good for the AICPA to change the code, because then the CPA would be getting into a totally different business and level of accountability to the client. If he wants to get out of his business, I have no problem."

The AAPFP's Cohen is against CPA–financial planners

accepting commissions. He sees the fee-only mode as not only more appropriate, but also one that has come to be expected of the CPA. "CPA fees for financial planning seem to be similar to fee structures for regular service," says Cohen. "Seventy-five to one hundred twenty-five dollars an hour represents the average hourly rate. CPAs already have clients oriented toward paying an hourly rate. Commissions are something they never really had. Right now, based on [the AICPA Code of] Ethics, they really can't do both. That's probably why some gave up being a CPA and went over into products."

Some CPAs have chosen to belong to those associations that allow them to practice business the way they choose. "We're a registered investment advisor, but we are not members of the AICPA because they've come out and said you shouldn't sell product," says Thomas Hart, CPA, principal of The First Continental Company in Toledo, Ohio (see Chapter 2). "The Ohio Society of CPAs said it was okay to sell product, so we've maintained our membership there. We do product sales—insurance, mutual funds—and use the commissions to offset our fees. We set up two companies: one to receive fees, which is the registered investment advisor; the other to sell product."

WALKING THE GRAY LINE

Some CPAs have avoided the issue of whether or not to accept commissions by choosing to walk the gray line between giving general financial advice (and not having to register with the SEC) and registering as a full-blown investment advisor.

"We've always been doing the same thing," says Terry O'Sullivan, principal of Moody, O'Sullivan and Company, a CPA firm in North Andover, Massachusetts. "We're not registered and don't give advice. We have a problem with the commission aspect of business."

Yet many of Moody, O'Sullivan's clients do seek out their counsel. "In our business," says Bruce Moody, "we're usually the one the guys go to first. We're the confidants of these clients. These guys don't have the capabilities of filling all the voids. We, as generalists, fill them."

Adds O'Sullivan, "After we refer this investment client to a professional, often that client will come back to us. Then, if we're asked a product-type question, we might hedge an answer by saying it fits the overall financial plan. It's a thin line between the two. We probably could do [personal financial planning]. But like any business, you identify strengths and go with them. Our strength is tax planning."

"We control uncontrollable individuals," explains Moody in describing how his firm goes a step beyond typical tax planning, teetering into the area of personal financial planning. "We represent wild-men entrepreneurs and try to make them security-conscious. If I have a strength, it's that I can control the entrepreneur. We take him when he is in a start-up mode and help him get financing. When he starts doing well, we put in a pension plan. If he wants estate planning, we refer him to a lawyer."

"Terry and I are both entrepreneurs," Moody continues. "We started our own business. We know what it's like to not get paid, not sleep at night. If you work for a Big Eight firm, you get a salary. There's a big difference between a guy who works his way to the top and one who starts his own business."

"One of the things we know is what we don't know. Everybody's running to do financial planning because that's where the money is. No one person can do everything. Terry and I don't just want $7,500 to do financial planning; we want rich clients at the end."

FINDING TIME
FOR THE SHIFT

In fact, one of the main concerns of many CPAs seeking to enter the world of financial planning without totally giving up their careers as public accountants is how to find time to do both.

"One of the problems is they don't have the manpower," observes Jerry Cohen, who, before creating the AAPFP, ran his own CPA–financial planning shop with Roy Weitz for about three and a half years, offering comprehensive financial planning to around a hundred clients. "Probably right now there are not enough CPA–financial planners to go around. Firms will have to take a period of some years in some cases to get the education to get a person started."

The education that most CPAs entering the financial planning flock opt for is the certified financial planner (CFP) designation from the College for Financial Planning in Denver, says Cohen. "A few states, like California and Colorado, have a curriculum through the state-run CPA foundation for certification in financial planning. The AICPA is also looking into adopting a program." But for now the CFP is the designation of choice.

"To deal successfully in financial planning" observes Delessert, "it takes a certain type of individual. You have to be able to convey that you have experience in what you are talking about. It's hard, damn hard, to find the right individual. That's been our biggest difficulty—finding the right people."

ROLLING OUT NATIONALLY

Seidman Financial Services is one of the more ambitious efforts of a public accounting firm to roll into the financial planning market. The effort grew out of Seidman and Seidman/BDO's 1985 acquisition of Bornhofft Financial Services, Inc. It was at Bornhofft that Christiane Delessert had made financial planning a profitable operation.

"They had five clients lined up for me when I went to Bornhofft," recalls Delessert, who served as the firm's president from 1983 until it merged with Seidman. The Bornhofft Financial Services operation moved to Seidman's offices at One Financial Center, across the street from Boston's Federal Reserve Bank in the South Station area of Boston, in August 1986. But although she had had operations running smoothly and, more importantly, profitably at Bornhofft, says Delessert, "It took us a full year to convince Seidman to go national."

For a year they stayed in the former Bornhofft offices. Finally, on July 1, 1986, "in theory" the operation was established. It began full operations in September 1986. "It was frustrating for me," she recalls. "Here I had set up Bornhofft—successfully. We merge; for one year I had to sell the idea to the partners. I was ready to move on."

Once Delessert convinced the 200 or so partners in Seidman to support a national rollout of Seidman Financial Services in Boston, New York, Detroit, Milwaukee, and Grand Rapids to start, their support was unflagging.

"I've had incredible support from partners," she says. "It's key. In an accounting firm, it's absolutely crucial to have support of partners. There are 200 partners in Seidman. There's an unbelievable commitment not to do it piecemeal. Obviously, they think it can be profitable; they've studied the Bornhofft model."

Perhaps a portion of the support comes from the fact that Seidman Financial Services operates as a limited partnership.

"We want the involvement of the partners," says Delessert. "Seidman Financial Services, Inc., operated as a corporation for four to six months, then we dissolved that and set up Seidman Financial Services Limited Partnership. Profit is distributed at the end of the year. Each partner in the firm has a number of units."

If Seidman Financial Services profits, the partners profit.

Delessert estimates that the average plan Seidman sells runs between $5,000 and $10,000. The market, she says, is "anybody we perceive having a need, who can afford the fee." Their highest client net worth is $30 million; the lowest $350,000.

SETTING UP A NETWORK
FOR IMPLEMENTATION

Even Seidman, with its vast resources and the commitment of 200 partners in its sister accounting firm, does not pretend to know it all. Since they do not sell product or accept commissions, they've had to set up a network of professionals who will implement their clients' financial plans once the planning stage is complete. Obviously they can rely on the network of accountants at Seidman and Seidman next door, but they also work with referrals of accountants outside the Seidman umbrella.

"I'm a specialized generalist," says Diane Lapon, one of three financial planners in the Boston office. "I have a lot of resources available to me. My approach is really only to understand the questions to ask."

And even though they are fee-only planners, like all seasoned financial planners the Seidman group must keep abreast of the latest products being offered so they can guide their clients through the maze.

"They'll need to have enough familiarity with products to send clients to various product suppliers," says Mark Bass, of

CPAs who enter the financial planning field. "Another alternative is to send them to a financial planner, which is where I get a significant part of my business. Or thirdly, somehow they will work an arrangement so that they will be remunerated. We've never done that." (Bass is based in Texas where the State Board of Public Accountancy has lifted its ban on commissions.)

"To me it's up to the client how he pays his professional," says Bass. "If the consumer has a great relationship to his CPA and the CPA says, 'Get into such and such a deal,' the consumer says, 'Look, I trust my CPA. Somebody's going to make money on this deal. It may as well be my CPA.'

"The ultimate judge of all of this is the client," Bass concludes. "If the client feels good about the CPA doing it, and it's legal for the CPA to do it, more power to him."

7 BUILDING SOFTWARE BY BUILDING RELATIONSHIPS

"Before the advent of the personal computer and reasonably integrated software, you would not be able to come close to break-even on the planning side," opines Joel Kocen, founder of Financial Goal Achievement Associates in Arcadia, California. "Were it not for a well-thought-out software system, I don't believe my business would exist."

One of the keys to successfully marketing a financial planning service, or any other service or product, lies in the tools the professional uses to develop those services or products. For the financial planner, software has been the Baedeker for the befuddled, the magic box that has lifted oft-struggling planners up and provided them with the productivity tool they needed.

"I don't think I could have done [financial planning] at all without software," says Marshall Wiley, a CPA in Fresno, California, who spends "about 30 to 40 percent" of his time doing fee-only financial planning. "I felt I was struggling. The software has helped me to get more organized and focused. It's also a tremendous learning tool. If you understood that software," says Wiley, referring to his financial planning software package, "you'd be a heck of a financial planner."

Steven Nielsen, an attorney and CPA who has been practicing financial planning in Sandy, Utah, for about a year, uses Softbridge Financial Planner software. "Currently I don't have a secretary," he says. "I would never have been able to do that if I didn't have Softbridge. At the moment, in these early stages, Softbridge is my secretary."

THE SEARCH FOR SOFTWARE

Financial planning software may increase productivity and bring more consistency, thus more quality control, to financial plans, but it is not a flawless antidote to the planner's problems. Too often, in fact, it adds to the problems. Companies peddling software products have gone in and out of business fast. And often the support that is promised is dismal at best.

The search for a quality software package that can help planners with their overall marketing efforts in building a practice takes time.

Steven Nielsen started using software in 1985. "I looked around at Softbridge, Leonard 5000, and Planman [by Sterling Wentworth Corporation]," he says. "In fact, I looked at Leonard and Planman at the suggestion of Softbridge."

It turns out that the fellow who recommended the comparison shopping was Cory Lowder, a CPA formerly in the Boston office of Deloitte Haskins and Sells. Before starting his own practice, Nielsen had been in the Salt Lake City office at the same Big Eight accounting firm. While at Deloitte, Lowder had been hired by Softbridge to do a quality check on the Softbridge package. "He ended up leaving Deloitte and going with Softbridge as one of their developers," says Nielsen.

When Nielsen began his search for software in his own shop, he turned to Softbridge because he knew the company. Lowder, however, "strongly suggested" he talk to some of the other software providers.

"As a regular part of our sales process, we try to help the prospective buyer with the decision," says Sam Guckenheimer, director of Softbridge's Financial Planning Business unit. "We try to be very open with information, and that sometimes means saying that 'based on the needs you describe, here are three things [products] to evaluate.' Obviously, if based on the needs you describe ours fits, we'll tell you that. But if it doesn't we'll tell you that, too."

It was not an easy selection process for Nielsen. The packages were priced similarly. "I could see pros and cons to all three," he recalls. "I began to flounder in my analysis. So I sat down to prepare my ideal financial plan. Then I based my decision on three criteria. First, how close is their current commercial product to this ideal? Second, which of the three could offer the ability to customize? And third, how responsive would the support of the company be to get me to that ideal the fastest?"

Ultimately, Nielsen chose Softbridge because he felt it would be "the most flexible. I liked the way I could go in and customize my own documents. In looking over Softbridge's history, I felt they had capital strength. They were younger in the industry but they put all their capital behind development. I sensed they were more responsive to users' needs. In the last two years, I think that has been born out."

THE SOFTBRIDGE PRODUCT: DRIVEN BY ECONOMIC AND CUSTOMER CLIMATE

Softbridge Microsystems Corporation began operations in 1983. In 1985, after researching the market, it began sales of its product—the Softbridge Financial Planner, a comprehensive personal financial planning software package for the IBM personal computer. The package uses a piece of technology developed by Softbridge called UNITY, which allows users to customize the system and make use of the Lotus 1-2-3 spreadsheet, Multimate word processing, and Informix database that make up the package.

Over the two years since the product has been offered, Guckenheimer estimates that Softbridge has doubled the capabilities of the system. "Some of those changes were driven by tax changes," he says, "much more by user suggestions and requests. We've had three to four enhancement updates a year for the user."

Nielsen is not the only user of Softbridge to cite the company's responsiveness and its capital strength as a reason for opting to go with Softbridge's product. (The company was heavily funded by venture capital funds when it began in 1983.) "We were with a smaller [software] company, but they just didn't have the capital," says Tim Evans, associate regional director of financial planning for Kidder Peabody and Company, Inc., in Atlanta, Georgia. Evans has also been impressed with Softbridge's responsiveness to his suggestions for improvement of the product. That never worked out with the smaller firm. They were always very defensive.

"I'm very impressed with their 800 number," continues Evans. "Sometimes when you call one of those numbers, you get somebody who assumes that you haven't read the manual. So far, that hasn't happened to me with them."

Softbridge doesn't have any plans to stop the 800 number support service, which Guckenheimer estimates has cost the company "well over $10,000 in phone bills during heavy periods," but it has started screening support calls to route them to area specialists. Before, it had rotated the calls. The routing to area specialists has allowed them to control the quality of the calls a little better.

"We're in the business of providing service to clients," says Guckenheimer. "The software is very important to their business, so we have to be responsive. It may be expensive, but it's an important part of the relationship we've built.

Softbridge has also allowed financial planners like Evans to incorporate more quality control into their planning efforts. "It allows us to produce some uniformity among plans," Evans says. "Granted, every client's different so every plan's different, but at least we're seeing some uniformity among some of the schedules, which leads to greater quality control, which hopefully will lead us to be more efficient and give us more time for marketing."

The customization aspect of the Softbridge Financial Planner has also been a marketing boon to those who provide services to financial planners. Janet Carhart is not a financial planner but provides data processing services to them through her Financial Planning Systems Corporation in Arlington,Virginia. "From my standpoint, the ability to customize documents is great. Everybody wants to have something that no one else on the street has. From my standpoint, that's incredibly saleable."

"Our clients have been enormously impressed with the quantitative data," says Joel Kocen, whose shop was one of the beta (test) sites for Softbridge. Kocen boasts having package number 0006. "It's the customization—to be able to pick and choose any number of quantitative schedules and write around them—that, by and large, has been absolutely excellent. We have clients who have moved out of town who keep us as planners. Our practice is growing literally around the country."

In short, it seems clear to Softbridge users that a good deal of client receptivity comes from the customization factor. By being able to incorporate their own words and style into the plans, planners are able to differentiate their practices and add that little something extra that gives clients a reason to believe in them.

That little something extra is called "relationship marketing."

RELATIONSHIP MARKETING

"Relationship marketing is very hot for everyone right now," observes Softbridge's Guckenheimer. "In the past you might have just sold insurance or mutual funds. But being a financial planner lets you build a relationship, and you can build in additional services, all of which makes you a credible advisor to the client."

"Capabilities and integrity are what interest clients," says Kocen. "They're not interested in how we work the alchemy in a black box."

Even when you're doing well, however, there's still fault to be found. There's a story Mickey Mantle likes to tell about his recent bout with chest pains that resulted in a short stay at a Texas hospital. While the Mick turned out okay, he had a dream while in the hospital that he died and found himself standing in front of Saint Peter at the gates of heaven.

"Name?"

"Mickey Mantle."

The Saint read down his list, then went to consult with a few other angels on the matter.

"We're sorry," he told the Mick, "but because of the life you led on earth, there's no place for you up here. . . . But while you're here, the guys want to know if you'll autograph these six-dozen baseballs."

Mickey Mantle's story comes refreshingly to mind when you talk to people who use the Softbridge Financial Planner. Without exception they are full of glowing praise, but it's always coupled with a criticism or two.

The interesting thing about Softbridge, however, and no doubt one of the reasons its users sing its praises, is that the company responds positively to customer criticism, sometimes incorporating suggestions in the enhancements of its software product that it regularly rolls out of the shop.

The same relationship marketing capabilities that Softbridge opens up for financial advisors are used by Softbridge in dealing with its users. "We made it as open a product as we could, as changeable and customizable by the individual user," says Sam Guckenheimer. "It gives the individual practitioner tremendous control. That's one of the key reasons people turn to us. The major force in our prioritization is giving the customer what he wants."

Customers have identified needs as diverse as needing commas in large numbers to be able to read them more easily and being provided with a less complex plan within Softbridge that can help them meet the needs of what Guckenheimer jokingly calls the "yuppies or retired couples not owning a lot of partnerships."

Softbridge put the commas in. And in 1986 it began "embedding" in its comprehensive planning package something called QuickPlan, which allowed financial planners to provide less comprehensive plans for their clients with less complex financial problems.

In early June of 1987, Softbridge rolled out QuickPlan as a separate product, selling it for $2,495, with an annual fee of $900 for planner support. QuickPlan can be upgraded to the more comprehensive Softbridge Financial Planner package for an additional $4,000. (Softbridge Financial Planner sells for $6,000, with an annual fee of $1,200 for planner support.)

"We don't see much use for QuickPlan," says Kidder Peabody's Tim Evans. "For us, a major asset of Softbridge is putting in a chart with sixteen assets and five liabilities and letting Softbridge crunch the numbers.

"We haven't found a QuickPlan yet," he continues. "There's no such thing as a quick plan. We tried it once or twice but really haven't made use of it. Our plans are pretty complicated. But if you're a planner with a client who has a W-2, a house, car, and a boat, then QuickPlan is the way to go."

Others, like Marshall Wiley, a CPA in Fresno, California, who spends "about 30 to 40 percent" of his time doing fee-only financial planning, swear by QuickPlan. "My experience is that Softbridge [Financial Planner] is extremely powerful. I probably don't use anywhere near its capabilities. I'm pretty much using QuickPlan.

"When I first bought it, it didn't have QuickPlan, but it did have different levels [of sophistication in plans]. People only read the short plans anyway," Wiley jokes. "I don't feel like a power user. I call them and they help me solve my problems."

INNOVATIVE MARKETING TO BUILD RELATIONSHIPS

But some planners who chiefly use the comprehensive Softbridge Financial Planner with their clients have found innovative marketing uses for QuickPlan. One planner who had been using the comprehensive package for several years decided to use QuickPlan to target a seminar market.

"Four weeks before the seminar, you send the twenty or so attendees a questionnaire and they give it back a week before the seminar," says the planner. "During the seminar, you give them back the plan and also address specific questions."

The planner finds this usage of QuickPlan a particularly effective tool in marketing financial planning services to corporations that might purchase it as a perk for their executives.

The reaction to the addition of QuickPlan to the product will continue to be mixed. Those planners who cater to more upscale clients with complex financial situations will find little use for QuickPlan. Those who are trying to provide sophisticated plans for middle-class clients who have straightforward needs and few complicated investments will find QuickPlan an economical choice.

At a time when tax reform has made highly commissionable products less available, financial planners are looking for that extra edge that can help them effectively market their services and build relationships with clients. To cost-effectively generate fees for plans, planners have searched for the best software to meet their needs. Many have faced a series of trial-and-error purchases resulting from a lack of due diligence in their software purchasing decision. Others have been treated to a Kafkaesque nightmare as they dared to seek help from a software support line.

But it is unquestionable that for planners to succeed in today's marketplace—particularly entrepreneurial planners who have set up their own small shops—effective, usable software is crucial. Many have found that their very existence depends on the continued use of good financial planning software.

"The system is by no means perfect," observes Joel Kocen about Softbridge. "There's no perfect system. But they're working at making it better and better. It would be impossible for me to start over again with a new system. They get pneumonia and I die."

PART THREE
TARGET MARKETING

A common key to successful marketing in many professional service fields like financial services is target-marketing, whether through direct mail advertising or by offering services tailored to specific markets, like women or the elderly. Zero in on a particular niche, tailor your services to its needs, and keep giving the market what it wants. The benefits are that you know whom to approach, and you place boundaries on that market. Rather than going after the world, you're after a specific segment of the world.

The Selkirk Correspondent is a sophisticated piece of direct mail software that professionals can use to track active clients and target prospective clients. Chapter 8 looks at the development of the Selkirk Correspondent and other direct mail software packages and how these can be used with a personal computer to target-market. It also examines how a company marketing "marketing" software can have problems targeting its own market, and whether or not a new owner of the software can succeed where its predecessor faltered.

As women enter the work force in increasing numbers and struggle to find equitable pay and positions with men as well as grapple with their concerns over money, they become a growing market for financial services professionals to target. Chapters 9 and 10 examine the women's market and the issues affecting it, then look at how Laurie McCormick, who runs a one-person financial planning shop in Boston, caters to a chiefly female client base.

The elderly are another group with unique financial planning needs. In Chapter 11, we look at Vern Woodrum, who came out of retirement to service this market. Woodrum thought he had retired from the financial world when he closed his insurance shop in Akron, Ohio. But when he resettled in Charleston, South Carolina, he found that more and more people sought out his fee-only financial advice. Woodrum knew his target market well, the elderly. His insight into the needs and fears of the elderly has allowed him to target that market successfully. Chapter 11 explores Woodrum's tactics in that marketplace.

8 DIRECT FROM THE SOURCE:
Using Direct Mail Software to Target Market

Financial Planning Advisors, Inc., is a six-year-old, fifteen-person financial planning firm based in Lexington, Massachusetts. The company, which was begun by John Reilly, CFP, also has branches in nearby Framingham and downtown Boston.

Like other financial planning shops, one of the ways Financial Planning Advisors has expanded its fee-plus-commission business over the past six years has been to run personal finance seminars once or twice a month. The seminars attract between thirty and a hundred prospective and current clients. The result has been not only increased business but also a potential record-keeping nightmare. Invitations to send out, names to be tracked according to interests and background, whether or not an invited guest attended—the paperwork is endless. At first Financial Planning Advisors ran its direct mail operation manually, trying to keep track of all the business and prospective business that was coming its way. But while business continued to grow, so did the paperwork.

TARGETING AN AUDIENCE WITH SOFTWARE

Opting for a more manageable system, Financial Planning Advisors turned to Selkirk Associates, Inc., a Boston-based software company that marketed the Selkirk Correspondent, a direct mail marketing management program that runs on personal computers. The $1,500 program ($1,850 with a day's customization and training on the software) allows Financial Planning Advisors to track each of its responses and tailor its mailings to the tastes and needs of the individual respondees.

The Selkirk Correspondent was introduced in January 1984 after having been tested in late 1983 at several "beta" sites. It was purchased in February 1987 by the Market Planning Group, a Boston consulting and software firm specializing in insurance and financial services. The company has retained *The Selkirk Correspondent* as the name of its product. Prior to purchasing the Correspondent, Market Planning Group had been one of its larger distributors, marketing a customized version of the software to the insurance industry.

"We run about one seminar a month," says Helen Reilly, vice president of marketing for Financial Planning Advisors.

"[The Correspondent] allows us to run one a month comfortably. In the past, we were able to run one a month, but it was a lot more disorganized.

"Basically, before using Selkirk, we were just doing everything manually. Everything was confining and chaotic. We had between 300 and 900 names to send to for each seminar. The names were just put on cards and stored in boxes. Using Selkirk, all the information goes onto [the software], whether or not they attended."

MANAGING THE
PRACTICE BEYOND
THE SEMINARS

In addition to its uses for seminars, the Correspondent software allows the members of Financial Planning Advisors to track their other clients. "Other people doing direct mail in the firm create their own client file. The program allows us to track specific interests on our internal database and sort by different characteristics," explains Helen Reilly.

"As we grow, [Correspondent] allows us to manage people beyond the seminars," she says. "We can also see if a name is already in our database, which helps in terms of nonduplication of effort."

Financial Planning Advisors runs its Correspondent software on a 20-megabyte hard disk, to which it has networked, through a Novelle system, fifteen Compaq Deskpro 286 computers. Several laser jet printers are kept busy printing out letters and other materials fed off the computers.

A PLETHORA OF
PROGRAMS NOW
AVAILABLE

Companies that target-market products and services to specific audiences—like many financial advisors—are blessed by the development and availability of programs like Correspondent. While direct mail marketing management software has been available for a long time to run on larger computers or to handle enormous databases with hundreds of thousands of names, it is only within the last four or five years that such programs have become readily available for use on personal computers.

"Boy, there really is a lot of direct mail software," says Craig Huey, president of Creative Direct Marketing Group, a full service, direct response advertising agency in Torrance, California. "It's overwhelming," says Huey, who is also publisher of the monthly twelve-page newsletter *Direct Response: The Digest of Direct Marketing.* "The key to it is determining what's good."

In late 1987, Huey tested 100 to 125 direct mail marketing management software programs to evaluate their effectiveness. He printed the results in his newsletter.

So far, the better programs still appear to be targeted to direct mail houses, which manage databases of names and addresses in the 100,000-plus region. For direct mail programs capable of handling these kinds of numbers, Huey says that people have "been happy" with, among others, NameBase and Pro-Mail.

Referring to the smaller business market, James A. Lunden, president of Software Marketing Associates, Inc., the marketer of Pro-Mail, says, "We've never solicited business in that direction." But he also says he's "thinking about marketing a separate program to that group."

Huey says that "if anybody knows about PCs, he could use DBase II or Paradox, a new [database software package] getting a lot of favorable publicity and comments."

As for the Selkirk system, he says, "I don't know if there's a verdict on that. The last reading was that it was good for small operators, but if you have a larger company, it really strains that software. If you're a company doing over 100,000 pieces a month or more, Selkirk is designed for a smaller operation."

PERSONALIZING MASS MAILINGS

While several types of list-management programs are available, for the smaller business operation most do not have the same potential impact on the overall marketing plan as Correspondent does.

The user of Correspondent can create detailed customer information records. A more attractive feature of the software, however, is that users can isolate customers with specific characteristics, based on all the information stored in their database. Using this information, users can create letters, invitations, or other correspondence personalized toward everybody within that specific group.

For example, Financial Planning Advisors has a ten-step financial planning process it takes each of its clients through. "We can track where each person in the system might be," observes Helen Reilly. "We can print a list of people at a certain stage. We can code it and draw a list out to customize it according to the way our system works in-house. That makes it a very nice fit for us. For a small database, it's perfect."

For its seminars, Financial Planning Advisors has, according to Reilly, "been sending out between 500 and 2,000 invitations a month." These names are gleaned from lists of prospective clients. Between thirty and one hundred people attend the seminars. The Correspondent software is then used to send out personalized follow-up letters to those who did and did not attend.

"It's an excellent thing in the way you can customize it," she says. "It's very useful for people trying to communicate with a growing population."

Correspondent has helped Financial Planning Advisors and other users hone their marketing skills. The software allows them to build up a database of information. Once that information is collected, they must determine what to do with it. The software does not make management decisions for them, but may help them see things in a new way or reorganize their business habits to market products and services more effectively.

"[The software] manages your information but doesn't improve your sales," observes Helen Reilly. "Our closing ratio has changed more as a result of our growth."

THE CORRESPONDENT COMPONENTS

Correspondent is made up of a database and a word processing system. Three different files make up the database.

The People file stores information on the people or things a company is keeping track of. In the case of Financial Planning Advisors, users can profile a customer's name, whether it is a person or a business, the address, and the customer's status in the financial planning process.

The Activity file in the database keeps track of the transactions that occur with each customer. Whenever Financial Planning Advisors sends a seminar invitation, places a telephone call, or gets a positive response to an invitation, that action can be recorded on the software.

The Event file can be used to schedule events that should happen in the future. If someone at Financial Planning Advisors sets up an appointment with a prospective client for two months from now, the software can not only record the transaction in the Activity file but also note in the Event file that in two months the meeting will occur. A user can then call up the Event file for any given week and have all the events that should occur that week spelled out.

Using the word processing capabilities, users can compose new documents or store boilerplate documents to be called up for use whenever it is appropriate.

The word processing and database systems are integrated, so users can call up names with specific characteristics from the database and print out the names on labels or directly onto envelopes. Users can also develop direct mail campaigns consisting of a series of follow-up letters that can be stored in the system and sent out when appropriate. The Correspondent software can then be used to generate reports on how mailings have performed.

The software operates on the IBM PC, PC/XT, PC/AT, or any IBM-compatible machine with at least 256 kilobytes of memory, a 10-megabyte hard disk, a monitor, and a letter-quality printer. Many companies prefer using laser printers because of their better quality and increased speed.

The capacity of the software in terms of how many names it can hold is determined by the size of the hard disk. "It can store up to 15,000 names," says Kathleen Pasley, president of Market Planning Group, referring to the 10-megabyte hard disk. "But you're only restricted by the size of your hard disk."

COMPETITIVE PC DIRECT MAIL SOFTWARE PRODUCTS

The Correspondent is not the only direct mail marketing software that's been marketed. About the same time Selkirk launched the Correspondent, other companies got into the fray.

In fact, Binary Systems, Inc., of Newton, Massachusetts, attempted to market two different versions of a direct mail marketing software package. Originally it marketed Executive List Management to users of Canon computers. It then adapted this software for IBM personal computers and called it Market Master. The sales were disappointing.

"If somebody wants to buy it we'll sell it," says Sheldon Kaplan, applications manager for Binary Systems. The software, which originally sold for $895 a pop, is now being softly peddled for $495, which, Kaplan insists, is no reflection on the quality of the software.

"We did sell it, but the field is kind of tricky," says Kaplan. "There's a lot of competition. It was a very tough thing and really didn't work out for us."

Binary Systems has successfully marketed fidelity bond rating software: CB Rater ($1,000) and Easy Rater ($2,500). They're used to "compute ratings for liability for losses uncovered for theft from employees," explains Kaplan.

Kaplan estimates that they probably sold a total of sixty-five Market Master and Executive List Management software packages, including those marketed by a distributor to insurance companies through N-Sure Systems, Inc., operating out of Monroe, Louisiana.

Kaplan is philosophical about the dismal sales of Binary's direct mail package. "We haven't had any inquiries [about Market Master] for a while. It could have been marketed better. It's a good program. . . . But with [Easy Rater and CB Rater] I knew who I was going after. With the [direct mail software] you have to have marketing follow-up. It's just different. [The market for ratings software] is not so amorphous a market, you know who you're trying to get to. I guess we could have sold Market Master, but there's only so much time. You have to go where you can make the most money."

In its attempt to sell the Selkirk Correspondent, the Market Planning Group will try to escape the irony of marketing "marketing" software with less than stellar results. But the question that remains to be answered is whether or not the Market Planning Group can market the software more effectively than Selkirk Associates.

TARGETING THE
SOFTWARE

At the time of Correspondent's sale to the Market Planning Group, Selkirk Associates had sold the package to just over 500 users. Does the Market Planning Group have the marketing savvy and financial muscle to sell the product?

"We feel it's critical to our success to market the product to targeted groups," says G. Wayne Harris, Market Planning Group's chairman. "We are trying to look for distributors specializing in specific industries. We'll give them the product at a discount, and they can do some minor customizing and sell it at whatever price they want."

"I think [Selkirk] made two major mistakes," says Harris. "One was a fragmented marketing approach. The other was they put a lot of money into R&D [research and development]."

"They were trying to come up with a minicomputer version of the product," adds David D. Taylor, vice president of Market Planning Group, who, along with Kathleen Pasley, the company's president, has worked with Harris in the insurance industry. "They put a lot of R&D all in one client. They were software people, not marketing people."

The Market Planning Group was formed in late summer 1984 as a consulting firm to the insurance industry. When they bought the Selkirk Correspondent in February 1987, they had been distributing the product to the insurance industry for just over a year.

"It's all bootstrap money," says Harris, when asked how the purchase of the Correspondent was financed. "We're a couple-of-year-old company with fifteen people. We've tended to our knitting in a sense by sticking with the insurance business because we knew the insurance business. If we had a lot more money, we'd expand."

In their year as a Selkirk distributor, Taylor estimates they sold fifty to seventy-five copies of the software. He thinks they can do even better as owners of the product. "[Selkirk] had twelve distributors and it seems only two really did something with it, and one was us," says Taylor.

"We've had it for two months and have added three distributors," boasts Harris. "There is a tremendous profit potential in this devil."

"Selkirk identified the key industries to go after but didn't have the horses to make it work," says Taylor.

As owner of the package, Market Planning Group is still in the early stages of marketing the software. The group has inherited the existing clients, to whom, the principals say, Selkirk Associates sent a letter explaining the shift in control.

Market Planning certainly has its work cut out for it in maintaining existing and securing new clients for its product. Many existing clients, including Helen Reilly at Financial Planning Advisors, were unaware that any shift had occurred.

SATISFYING
A MARKET NICHE

There is little doubt, however, that the Market Planning Group is sitting on a potential gold mine of a product, if customer satisfaction is any judge.

"Our prospecting is much more defined now," says Dennis Lofton, president of Jones Hill and Mercer, Inc., an insurance firm in Savannah, Georgia. "The software's really key. The old financial planning deal was to get as many appointments as possible. The software helps you find out where your prospects are. The reports it generates analytically give you a whole lot better way to look at things rather than hit or miss."

One of the earliest users of Correspondent was Softbridge Microsystems Corporation, that stalwart of financial planning software based in Cambridge, Massachusetts. In fact, it was using it back in the development stages of Softbridge.

In early 1984, Correspondent was being used to help Softbridge conduct its market research. It's no small testament that a software company of Softbridge's stature still uses Correspondent for its direct mail capabilities.

"Yes, we still do use it," says Alan Levin, Softbridge's director of marketing. "We've used it a long time. It's a good example of when you've got something that works, you don't get rid of it. Once you get it, if it works, keep it."

Softbridge now uses the software to track leads and to track telemarketing interactions.

"We mainly use it to generate labels and customize letters to people," says Levin. "We've never run out of space. We have over 10,000 names in there easily."

"[Selkirk] is relatively simple to use," he adds. "There's a difference between easy to use and easy to learn. This one's easy to use." Levin explains that software that is easy to learn usually is learned quickly but not very useful for very long. On the other hand, with software that is easy to use, you have to think about what you are doing, but it continues to do what you need it to do.

"We've been doing a lot of direct mail for about five years," says Dennis Lofton, whose company purchased Correspondent software about a year ago. "We had another system, but I like this one a lot better. It's a pretty nifty little system."

9 WOMEN AND MONEY:
Understanding the Market

In 1987, the International Association for Financial Planning (IAFP) released a survey of Americans' attitudes about money. Buried in the data collected from 1,014 Americans was the curious observation that "women are markedly less optimistic than men when it comes to finances and are likely to be more concerned about this area."

Among the findings of the survey were the following:

- By a 46- to 30-percent margin over men, women say future generations will be worse off.
- Women are more likely than men to say that it's harder now to pay bills and have money left over than it was several years ago. Higher income women (those making more than $50,000), the survey noted, are 50 percent more likely than men to say 1987 will be harder than 1986.
- Additionally, 50 percent of women making over $50,000 are concerned about outliving their retirement money, a shocking 42.5 percent more than men.

What can a financial services professional make of these statistics? Are there opportunities to target a women's market that surpass anyone's expectations? If so, what must the professional keep in mind when approaching that market?

But more importantly, how do these figures from the IAFP survey help professionals understand the women's market more effectively?

UNDERSTANDING THE WOMEN'S MARKET

There is no question that everyone, not just women, appears to be very concerned about the country's economy. In *Money* magazine's annual "Americans and Their Money" survey published in November 1986, 78 percent of those surveyed expressed concern over the $2 trillion federal deficit.

In fact, in its November 1985 readership survey, *Working Woman* magazine found that among its affluent, well-educated readership "a startling one of two worries about ending up destitute." Sadly, the article continued, "these fears may be fueled by reality, for one out of five women sixty-five and over actually does live in poverty."

This "bag-lady syndrome," as the magazine labeled it, did not disappear with the following year's survey. One thirty-six-year-old professional earning more than $60,000 wrote in response to the 1986 *Working Woman* survey, "I gravely fear not having sufficient funds to support myself through the ripe old age I plan to live to," a response very much in keeping with the IAFP findings about outliving one's retirement funds.

"That concern is part of the American baggage today," says Bonnie Siverd, contributing editor to *Working Woman* and author of *The Working Woman Financial Advisor* (Warner Books, 1987). "But I don't buy [the findings of the IAFP survey] as a yardstick to say that those are indications of pessimism. It is true that there is a bag-lady syndrome out there. Women *will* say they are concerned about retirement security. But two real concerns are that we earn less than men do and we outlive you guys. Those are two nuts-and-bolts, dollars-and-cents realities. We haven't been there that long. Confidence comes from experiences. And our experience as working women is not as great as working men's."

Some indicators suggest that the parity between the value placed on men's and women's work is getting better, but it's still not equitable. According to the Census Bureau, from 1970 to 1984 the median income of women versus men grew from 59 to 64 cents on the dollar, but that's still a shamefully disparate proportion, particularly coupled with the fact that 60.9 percent of all households headed by single women with young children were classified as poor, up from 57.5 percent in 1978. Female-headed households comprised nearly half (48.1 percent) of all poor households in 1985 in the United States.

The fact that pay discrimination based on sex is illegal under Title VII of the Civil Rights Act of 1964 and the Equal Pay Act of 1963 makes these Census findings even more deplorable.

And, while the gap between men and women in longevity may be narrowing, the fact is that in 1983 women on average still outlived men by more than seven years, according to the National Center for Health Statistics. The only reason the gap seems to be narrowing is because of increased deaths of women smokers due to lung cancer and pulmonary disease. (Interestingly, working women appear to be healthier than nonworking women, according to statistics compiled by *American Demographics* magazine.)

What's even more shocking is that retired women—those over sixty-five years of age—according to 1986 statistics of the

Older Women's League, have average annual incomes of about $6,000, compared to $10,000 a year for retired men. This is partly because of the lack of pension income going to many older women, a fact that ideally will change as more and more women enter the executive suite.

THE REALISM OF THE WOMEN'S MARKET

"Women are more realistic," says Judith Briles, CFP, when asked to explain the IAFP survey findings. "I haven't talked to anyone under forty-five who has any comfort level about Social Security. By the time we get to the year 2015, it's zappo, because baby boomers are all there and not replenishing the population."

As a result, fewer people are paying more money into the Social Security pool to support a large population of retired baby boomers. "It's a sophisticated Ponzi scheme," says Briles, who is the author of *Money Phases: The Six Financial Stages of a Woman's Life* (Simon and Schuster, 1984). Briles, who is forty-two years old, says she doesn't count on anything coming from Social Security.

If there is indeed an outlook of pessimism, perhaps some of it is fueled by persistent media reports on the dismal plight of women in society.

Lenore Weitzman, author of *The Divorce Revolution* (Macmillan, 1987), reports that, on average, after a divorce, women experience a 73 percent decline in their standard of living while men experience a 42 percent increase. What's more, the average child support ordered paid by a father comes to $200 a month for two children. But 53 percent of noncustodial parents do not comply with the court order for child support payments. Those men making between $30,000 and $50,000 a year are as likely to be in default as those earning $10,000, according to Weitzman.

Underearning to protect a husband's ego is also a problem. In *The Crisis of the Working Mother* (Summit Books, 1986), author Barbara J. Berg addresses the issue of underearning on the part of working mothers: "Underearning may also be an effort to assuage guilt about working. Some working mothers hold themselves back so that they will not threaten their husband's earning power."

Berg concludes that "it is really irresponsible for any mother to be financially ignorant or incompetent." But the fact remains that women historically have not been privy to the same esteem given men in the workplace—either in terms of ego-stroking or in terms of dollars.

WOMEN'S
SELF-PERCEPTION

In the *Money* magazine poll, more women than men (58 to 41 percent) rated themselves adept at managing money. But more men than women (52 to 40 percent) view managing money in long-term strategic terms. According to the survey, women tend to be short-range managers: 61 percent (vs. 48 percent of the men) said that being a good money manager meant finding bargains, and 69 percent (vs. 56 percent of the men) said it meant staying out of debt.

The women responding to surveys like those of *Working Woman* and *Money* do not necessarily reflect the attitudes of all women. Michele Morris, business editor of *Working Woman*, admits, "Women who respond [to our surveys] are an elite group. They are making money, are in control, and have a sense of optimism that others may not have."

The average income for individual readers of *Working Woman* hovers around $37,000; combined household income averages $59,000.

"To generalize about women is really hard," says Siverd. "This [IAFP] survey makes me uncomfortable because I have no idea who these women are. The only thing I would not want to see happen is for somebody to take anxiety about the future and translate that into anxiety about money, financial management, and ultimately incompetence. It's true you can have reservations abut the future, but that does not have to mean you think you're doing a bad job now. I've seen that leap happen so many times in so many male brain cells. There is a deep and abiding fear of the future. But it's perfectly possible to live with that looming on the horizon and not be as pessimistic as is suggested by those numbers."

Siverd's observations seem borne out by a survey released in February 1987 that was completed for *The Wall Street Journal* by the Roper Organization, called "The American

Dream: A National Survey." The results showed that while significantly more men than women (37 to 28 percent) felt that dream was "very much alive," women placed themselves further along the road to the American Dream than did men. On a scale of 1 to 10, women tallied in at 5.9, while men came in at 5.7. Both men and women believed equally that they would ultimately reach 8.2 on a scale of 10 on the road to the American Dream.

FINANCIAL SERVICES FIRMS INCREASINGLY TARGET WOMEN

Recognizing the potential of the women's market and women's thirst to continue on that dream-filled road, many financial institutions have already begun targeting them as powerful earners in need of financial advice and products.

"Since I've been here," says Michele Morris, who has been with *Working Woman* for three years, "more and more financial services firms are targeting women. Women may be too busy, but they are not afraid. They are looking for concise direction, not just for advisors but explainers. They want someone who can cut through the verbiage and list choices so they can make a decision. Among women, there is a hunger and a thirst for more information and to simplify and streamline things. They really want to get control."

"Working women and mothers feel busy," confirms Siverd, but they also "feel a need for expertise. We've found an enormous interest on the part of women to find financial professionals. But too often they are talked down to, just not explained things."

In *Working Woman's* December 1986 survey, a shocking two-thirds responded affirmatively to the statement "Financial advisors don't take female clients as seriously as male clients." Seven out of ten responded affirmatively to the statement "Given their equal competence, I'd rather consult a woman financial advisor than a man."

Right off, this presents a marketing hurdle for all financial planners—a tremendous one for male financial planners.

"Women are interested and do want help," says Siverd. "But one of the first things financial advisers have to do when targeting women is to get over the hump of mistrust and skepticism. If [a bad experience with a financial advisor] didn't happen to them, then it happened to a friend. Women have gone through too many years of being patted on the head and having their husbands pitched to.

"Women would respond to a financial planning concern that pushed the right buttons. That might be asking, 'What will you be eating when you're seventy-two? Will you be warm and well fed in your old age?' There is fear that it will be tough down the road. This could sound patronizing, but it doesn't have to. It's a matter of packaging."

The second hump financial advisors must get over in marketing to women, according to Siverd, is to get them to feel comfortable enough to tell the truth. "Women often hate to ask for help, and they feel more comfortable asking any kind of question to a woman. You have to let a potential woman client know she has a brain and can identify problems on her own. It's not holding the woman's hand and saying, 'Dear, dear, there's nothing to worry about,' but, 'You do need a sounding board and I can provide that.' [The financial advisor is] not a shoulder to cry on or a big daddy. The woman wants to fix it for herself. It's almost like saying, 'You already have the goal; we can brainstorm together for how to get from here to there.'"

"Women want information without a string attached to it," adds Judith Briles. "Firms need to go back to the old-fashioned method of establishing a relationship instead of immediately saying, 'Let's put your $5,000 here.'"

"Emotions lag reality," explains Briles. "The reality may be that women are doing well financially, but emotionally they still feel exposed. . . . Too often it's a fact that the mind has not caught up to your success. The financial advisor can first say, 'Yes, you feel this way, but on paper you have money and can continue to grow. We can work together.'"

10 WORKING WOMAN: *How One Woman Advisor Targets the Women's Market*

"In the past, women were raised to think that we didn't have to know about finances, that we would be taken care of," says Laurie B. McCormick, CFP, who runs financial planning and investment seminars for women as a service of her one-person financial planning shop, McCormick Associates.

"Some women still are waiting for 'Mr. Right' at forty-five. No one has spent time with them to say there are no guarantees, no one's going to take care of you."

If ever there was someone who understood that there are no guarantees, it's Laurie McCormick. Before beginning McCormick Associates in the tony Beacon Hill neighborhood of Boston, McCormick did her time as everything from a sales assistant at Merrill Lynch to a stockbroker at Thomson McKinnon.

McCormick went to Thomson McKinnon in 1977. It was there that she was first introduced to financial planner and personal finance writer Venita VanCaspel, who put on some seminars for Thomson McKinnon clients. McCormick is a VanCaspel disciple and bases much of her seminar presentation and financial planning approach on VanCaspel's work. "The bible for me is Venita VanCaspel," says McCormick. "I use Venita VanCaspel's books. Her format is simple; it's to diversify."

When VanCaspel came to town in 1977 to put on the seminars, McCormick recalls, "I spent a lot of time getting [her] on television, radio, and in the newspapers. She came back in 1978 and did another seminar for us. I got all the leads from that seminar and hired a Kelly Girl, who made sixty appointments for me."

Smooth sailing so far. McCormick went on to become in 1979 one of the first women in the New England region to earn her CFP (certified financial planner) designation. In April 1979, she left Thomson McKinnon and opened up her own shop, clearing her security sales through Investment Management and Research. She located her office at 6 Faneuil Hall Marketplace, an elegantly restored shopping area near the financial district in Boston.

"Everyone came with me," says McCormick of her clients at Thomson McKinnon. That in itself was no small feat. "I put the corporation first, as one who is honest would do," she says, recalling that she gave notice on a Friday. "I didn't send out my client letters until Monday. They [people at her office] called all my people on Saturday."

But perhaps sixty-five people followed her to the first incarnation of McCormick Associates. She was mostly selling mutual funds at the time. "I did everything Venita did because I followed her book. The office manager [at Thomson McKinnon] had said, 'I don't know what you're doing, but I want you to sell 50 percent stock.'" That solidified her decision to go it on her own.

Soon McCormick had the lesson about no guarantees in life laid out for her in quick, tough terms. The lesson manifested itself in the performance of one of her non–mutual fund products.

"One of my investments was Petro-Lewis [oil and gas limited partnerships]," she says. "In 1980 Petro-Lewis was deciding to divide up its regions. In April or May of 1980, they asked me to become the regional vice president for New England. I really agonized for six months. They offered me a very nice position. No one ever really had offered me anything before. Petro offered me a very nice package."

In October of that year, she accepted the position.

She sold her first company to a woman whom she trained. "She took over my clients, and after a year, she put the company in her own name."

As regional vice president for Petro-Lewis, McCormick was constantly on the road putting on public seminars for those who were selling its products. "I was out of financial planning for four years and into wholesaling."

Then Petro-Lewis's investment picture began to suffer. Ultimately they suspended sales. "In February 1981, they closed seven of our offices," says McCormick, whose office was among those closed in February. "Six months later they closed the rest."

"I had thirty job offers," she says. "But I decided never to work for anyone else. I decided to go back to what I loved— financial planning."

McCormick opened up her second office in August 1984, on Beacon Hill at the corner of Mt. Vernon and Charles, just down the street from where television's private eye "Spenser" used to have his firehouse apartment and a few blocks up from where Sam Malone and Norm hang out in the "Cheers" bar.

To date she has about 135 clients, 80 percent of whom are women.

CAPTURING FEMALE
CLIENTS WITH SEMINARS

To capture female clients, McCormick prospects with her strength—public speaking, a skill she picked up when she was with Petro-Lewis. "When I was with Petro-Lewis I averaged abut 200 public seminars a year," she says. The seminars are "a lot of fun," says McCormick. "I haven't had one person fall asleep yet."

In November 1984, she offered the first seminar for free. "About nine people came. She got those nine as the result of a direct mail advertisement about the seminar. Three of them became clients. "I convert a third to 50 percent of every seminar, no matter the price or how small or large the seminars are," she says.

She started charging $30 for her seminars around the spring of 1985. She raised that to $60 in September 1985 and finally to $95 in September 1986. "The reason I charge is if you don't charge, they don't show up. They have to commit themselves and you have to give them a dollar value. It's a commitment to show up."

The $95 seminar fee includes a two-part, four-hour seminar, an optional one- to two-hour consultation, and a two- to four-hour follow-up investment seminar. About 70 percent of the attendees take advantage of the consultation.

"In the seminars I use an overhead projector, transparencies, a white board, and handouts. Three visual aids help to keep the interest going. I go over what inflation has done to the dollar since 1900, so people realize that keeping their money in a bank isn't the best thing. I go over investment options, a five-page list of investment terms. Then I give specific examples of investments. I bring them from the high-risk end to the low-risk end in any investment.

"I'm very humorous in the meeting. I make light of a very intimidating subject."

The outcome, McCormick hopes, is that her audiences will learn to coordinate their financial goals. "I tell them how to diversify into different areas to accomplish their goals," she says. "I have to keep quite general, because I don't know who's sitting in the audience."

At the end of the seminar, McCormick hands out a critique sheet on which she asks not only for comments on the presentation but also for the names and addresses of people she should contact about future seminars. As a result she captures a list of excellent prospects for future business.

"Y'know I got it all thought out," she says. "Keep on prospecting."

While her list of qualified leads numbers in the area of 800, McCormick relies mostly on small advertisements in *The Boston Globe*, which run about two weeks before her seminars are offered. Her ad cries out

FINANCIAL PLANNING & *INVESTING* FOR WOMEN

She promises the attendees will learn

- What investments are right for you using the new Tax Reform Act
- Where to invest your IRA, Keogh, and IRA Rollover
- How to acquire the $500,000 estate
- How to effectively use Dollar Cost Averaging
- How to achieve FINANCIAL INDEPENDENCE

A phone number is given to reserve a spot. In small print at the bottom of the ad she notes that she sells securities through Dallas-based Southmark Financial Services.

A small black-and-white photo of McCormick appears in the ads. "I put a picture on the ad because I think a picture draws more. When I talk about money, I want to see who the person is who's advertising. If I have [a picture] in front of me, I can say, 'Gee, the eyes look honest . . . whatever."

"I get about eighty to a hundred calls from the ads," she says. At $2,600 per ad, she admits that that's a lot per lead, "but I just want people to come to the seminar."

Very rarely will she do any direct mail. She never buys mailing lists of names to invite to the seminars.

McCormick has met with some curious calls from men who see her newspaper advertisements. "I do get men calling. I get phone calls from men who say, 'You're discriminating.' I say, 'Yes.' But I do follow-up seminars for both men and women. I can't really advertise for women only and then have men [attend the seminars].

"I found out that a lot of women think men know more than they do. I alleviate that intimidation. Men have been raised to know about money. If women are going to live longer [than men], then they are going to manage most of the assets in the world. They have to be educated. It's not scary; it's easy."

All of McCormick's seminars are held at the Wellesley (Massachusetts) Community Center. "One thing I should do is to branch out from Wellesley," she admits. But while she realizes she "really should go to other places," her days with Petro-Lewis leave the idea of going on the road an unattractive option.

Besides, she says, "I can't do everything. I market myself, do the seminar, due diligence, consultation, implementation, and keep on top of investments. And I have to service my clients when they call."

Not surprisingly, she has booked all her rooms for seminars at the Wellesley Community Center well over a year in advance.

SERVICING A BROAD CLIENT BASE

McCormick's clients range from those who make $10,000 a year to one who makes in excess of $120,000. Some of the couples she counsels make more than $200,000 in combined income.

"I'm there for all income levels. Sometimes it's frustrating, but I've committed myself to helping everybody. My frustration comes out of the fact that here I am starting out all over again, while I think I should be further ahead of where I am." Still, she showed a profit in her first year in the new business. And she has scrambled back to start her second profitable financial planning firm relatively unscathed by the demise of Petro-Lewis.

McCormick, who began targeting a woman's market in November 1985, attributes one-third of her income to fees from consultation and plan preparation, the remaining two-thirds from commissions on products sold to clients. Her seminar fees go toward paying her seminar expenses. With fifteen to twenty people at each seminar, "the $95 doesn't even cover my costs," she admits.

While the woman's market appears to be keeping her busy

preparing and implementing plans, she sees other potential avenues of profit. "I would like to train financial planners to use my seminar," she says. "A lot of people flounder. They don't know which direction to go. My approach works. It's consistent."

"I'm more than willing to train people for a fee. I'd love to do that. If it could make money, great."

11 GRAY POWER:
Targeting an Elderly Market

Many planners target-market. Some go after doctors, others after women or Fortune 500 corporate executives, still others after professional athletes. Some go after anyone they perceive to be upwardly mobile.

Vern Woodrum, however, wants an older group as his client base—a market he thinks he can really understand.

It began in 1979 when Woodrum retired from a successful career running his own pension management firm in Akron, Ohio. "I decided to hang it up and went to Florida," recalls Woodrum, who in personality and demeanor is a cross between a sage Walter Cronkite and an acerbic Walter Brennan.

Once he got to Florida, Woodrum grew frustrated quickly. "All the streets were moving parking lots," he says. So when a friend invited him up to consider Columbia, South Carolina, as a home, he was easily tempted. As soon as he saw Columbia, he knew that was the place he wanted to be. "The azaleas were blooming. It was beautiful," he recalls. Soon, however, a marriage had Woodrum relocating to Charleston—about 110 miles away from Columbia—which was the home of his new bride.

In spite of his retirement, Woodrum opened up a fee-only financial planning office in Charleston in 1982. "I think word got out, because I started getting [as] clients people who needed fee-only planning," he says "I was making money in spite of myself."

While the opening of that practice might have spelled the end to an ungainful retirement, it also gave Woodrum an insight into a particular market that seemed to be going untapped, namely, people like himself. "I found out where my niche is, I think," says Woodrum. "The majority of my clientele is over age fifty."

TRYING INNOVATIVE
MARKETING TECHNIQUES

For a while, Woodrum was offering planning services to a condominium retirement village in Charleston called Cooper Hall.

"I was recommending the retirement place to a lot of clients," he recalls. "For many, a big house becomes a drain. It's an expensive retirement community, but they could buy a unit for $60,000, and that would include the services of a nurse and the use of a spa."

Woodrum had all the plans ready for offering a free initial interview with his Resource Development Corporation in a cooperative venture with Cooper Hall.

"I made up a brochure and talked to the owner, who lives on the premises," says Woodrum. "He thought it was terrific and was going to promote it." The brochure was attractively prepared with Cooper Hall's logo on the cover above the words *Financial Planning*. Inside, the copy explained to the residents that Cooper Hall had obtained the services of Resource Development Corporation, registered with the Securities and Exchange Commission as investment advisors. "Private and personal financial advisory consultations will be provided at their office on the premises."

Everything was set for Woodrum to keep hours at an office provided by Cooper Hall. The situation presented him with an ideal opportunity to tap into his target market. But all did not go smoothly.

"He [the owner] was going to provide me with an office, but he wanted me to move in there [to one of the Cooper Hall units]," says Woodrum. "The principle [of the planning service] went across, but it didn't succeed only because the owner of the complex was attempting to sell apartments through me and I didn't go for it. It put me in a compromising position, and I backed off. It would have been the same as a commission— and I won't even let someone take me to lunch. The whole concept has almost fallen apart now as a result of my not moving in."

Woodrum says he does have one client who lives in the complex and perhaps four more who came to him in one way or another as a result of the thwarted effort.

TEACHING CLIENTS TO MANAGE

To attract new clients, Woodrum will run occasional free information sessions. "I don't call them seminars," he says. "I think the word is overworked. Instead I say we're having a little breakfast meeting. I usually invite twelve to fifteen people."

After the initial free consultation, when people are interested in becoming Woodrum's clients, he signs them to a contract that lasts only three months. "It says, in effect, it will take three months for a complete plan," says Woodrum. "At the end of the three months, I tell them they're going to monitor their own plan. I say, 'You're intelligent, you know how to do it.' I'm teaching them to be their own manager.

"Normally after three months, they don't want to let go. So I put them on a maintenance contract for another three months. About 70 percent go to that. They all can handle it, but some don't want to. Normally a person of my age or older doesn't know which way to turn. How are they going to get this information?"

One way, it appears, is for them to hire someone like Woodrum. "People need a good asset manager to advise them, because bank returns on trust funds are dismal," he says.

But it's not just in the area of asset management that Woodrum thinks his target market needs advice. He says, "I had a friend call me from southern Ohio. He said, 'Vern, my daughter is saying maybe I ought to turn over my assets now to avoid probate.' I asked him how much we were talking about. He was talking about an estate of $15 million that he had made from strip mining in the South.

"I told him to give her a million and keep the rest. I said 'If you give it away to her she's going to forget where it came from. The difference between an old man and an elderly gentleman is how much money he has in his pocket.' Now instead of saying, 'Dad, we're having dinner—can you go upstairs?' she'll say, 'Dad, would you stay for dinner?' "

Since Woodrum really believes that in many cases children do take advantage of their parents, he advises his older clientele to leave nothing to question in matters of how their money will be handled or how they will be cared for should that service become necessary.

"I tell them," says Woodrum, " 'If you don't make the decision about what you want done, then what happens to you is your own fault. When you look at costs, it's likely that the kids are going to put you in a dismal nursing home.' I play to that seed of doubt."

Woodrum believes he has a solution to the problem, and he recommends it freely to his clients. He tells them that they should make a provision in their will that basically says this: "If either I or my spouse should be unable to manage our affairs, then I want a special power of attorney given to my minister or someone I see every day. That will continue even if I become senile."

Woodrum explains that the person holding the power of attorney will "immediately take control of your assets so no one can steal them." But even before this happens, Woodrum explains, "the couple has gone to a church group or whatever and said, 'We want a couple to come live with us. We will pay [an agreed-upon amount per month] and provide a home and meals.' As a further check, the couple is going to pay the church $200 a month for someone to come down once or twice a month to make sure they're being taken care of.

"Now you have checks and balances. This way the couple can stay together in their own home. Now you've made your decision about what's going to happen with your life when you get older. That's something a younger planner would have no idea is a problem."

SURVIVING WHILE SELLING SERVICES IN A SMALL MARKET

Woodrum has a clear handle on his target market. The growth of his fee-only practice, however, will in his own estimation, be limited because of the size of the Charleston area. "Charleston is around 250,000 people," he says. "I think the base I'm working from is not big enough. You're limited in what you can earn."

Woodrum also perceives that it's very difficult for a fee-only planner to make it without struggling in the early years. "Unless you have another source of income, don't get into fee-only planning," he adivses. "I understand that an attorney, a CPA, or any professional working on fee realizes they're going to go a while before making money. If you're willing to go through a starvation period, then go ahead and do it." Woodrum's other income comes from the pension he receives from the time he ran his own firm in Akron.

Woodrum has successfully targeted the over-fifty market in Charleston, South Carolina, at least in part because he himself is in that over-fifty category. As a result, he thinks he's better able to recognize the market's needs and desires.

"It's a different breed," he explains. "Our interests are much different from younger people's. They're interested in career-building, while we may be winding down. They're building assets. Mine are built. They may be building a family. Mine's grown."

Since Woodrum believes the needs of younger clients differ substantially from and often conflict with those of their parents' generation, he says, "I try to gear my practice to those who are older. I feel very strongly that children take advantage of their parents, so I don't feel I can cater to both client bases effectively. The problems are a lot different."

Because of his target-marketing to an older market, Woodrum has developed solutions to problems other planners might not even think about. For instance, he says, "I have a whole list of doctors who will accept Medicare figures. If you don't ask your doctor, you get the higher fee. It's the old adage, 'Them that don't ask, don't get.'"

PART FOUR
THE PRODUCT
PRESENTATION

Product or service presentation may seem the simplest of marketing functions, but in fact it is full of complex decisions that can make the difference between success and failure in the financial services marketplace.

If you've got a great service business and you know that it adds something truly new to the marketplace, but the collateral material (brochures, reprints, fliers) you give to prospective clients about your company are schlocky, you're lost. The presentation of the product or service in a sophisticated, appropriate manner is crucial.

Corporate identity entails not only coming up with a logo and name for a company but also making sure that they appropriately reflect the nature of that company. In Chapter 12, you'll discover how two different companies—one an insurance provider, the other a financial planning shop—went through complete graphic make-overs. You discover the costs involved plus just how difficult the task of working with a designer to come up with the appropriate look can be, especially when many partners in the firm must reach agreement. The results, however, can be dramatic.

Advertisements blanket the newspapers and magazines today. Every ad exec from every publication is after the financial services marketplace to take ad space. In Chapter 13, you'll see how Weston Group in Wellesley, Massachusetts, worked with an advertising executive to come up with an innovative ad campaign that truly stands out. From ad concept to cost of the ad and the ad exec, you'll see how Weston's principals learned how to use advertising effectively and how to measure the results by looking at more than just how many direct calls they got from a specific ad.

Public relations and relationships with the press are crucial to the success of any financial services firm. Chapter 14 examines how the financial services professional can use public relations to make the business grow, how public relations differs from advertising and other marketing techniques, and what you should expect from a solid public relations campaign. Chapter 15 examines how financial services professionals can achieve a strong working relationship with the print media. Based on information from financial professionals who are consistently used as sources, reporters from *USA Today*, *Money* magazine, and other publications, and public relations pros, the chapter lays out the basic dos and don'ts for establishing long-lasting, mutually respectful press relationships.

Long thought of as a way to maintain customer interest, newsletters are growing in use by financial services professionals. Chapter 16 explores how a financial advisor in Tennessee profitably publishes his own newsletter, which is distributed each month to active and prospective clients. Chapter 17 takes a look at the many imprint newsletter publishers around who will write and print the newsletters and imprint your logo on the masthead. Professionals who run the imprint companies, and financial services professionals who have used them, give you the information you need to make a cost-benefit analysis of these services vs. publishing your own. In either case, the newsletter is an unsurpassed method of keeping your name in front of the client every month and maintaining strong client loyalty.

The final chapter in Part Four explores an opportunity that has presented itself of late, which results from large financial services companies, rolling out sophisticated advertising campaigns that emphasize comprehensive financial planning. Chapter 18 looks specifically at the impact the John Hancock "Real Life/Real Answers" campaign has had not only on John Hancock but also on the many financial services providers who are not members of the John Hancock family. This chapter explores the concept of "latch-on" marketing, in which the smaller provider benefits the awareness built by the larger company's expensive campaign.

12 CORPORATE IDENTITY:
The Look That Works

Undergoing a graphic make-over by coming up with a new name or logo can involve more than just a face-lift. It can push you to focus on who you are and what you want to offer through your company, considerations that all too often fly out the window in the hectic dealings of day-to-day business.

"Ventura County is a lot of small towns clumped together," says Craige Campbell, CFP, who was formerly a vice president with IFP Advisors, Ltd., in Ventura, California. "In the whole county, there are maybe two financial planners in the Registry [of Financial Planning Practitioners, a listing of planners who meet specific educational and experiential criteria]."

"We felt there was a great opportunity to be in the forefront of the financial planning community from an advisory standpoint," recalls Campbell, who now runs his own shop, Campbell and Associates, in Solana Beach, 20 miles north of San Diego.

But IFP had a problem. In addition to the financial planning it was providing its clients, it was also providing products, which ranged from securities and real estate to mortgages and insurance.

Campbell, who earned his bachelor's degree in financial services at San Diego State University, agreed with the three principals in the company, Wayne Fleischer, John Haggerty, and Nicholas Gibasthat, that it was time for a more appropriate identity for IFP—one that would put financial planning at the forefront and segregate the various product companies from the financial planning process.

DECIDING WHAT'S NEEDED

The three principals formed Harbor View Companies to handle product and decided to place the financial planning responsibilities under the IFP Advisors roof. To do this, they wanted a new logo that was more appropriate for IFP.

"We felt the [IFP] logo we had was a little ambiguous," says Campbell. "We thought about changing the name, but decided existing clients knew it, and didn't feel it was all that bad. Our public relations guy felt that alphabet names tend to be associated with financial companies anyway."

Martin Seifert, IFP's public relations person, introduced

them to Marsha Johnson, an artist who runs Traditions Design Group in Ventura. "We sat down with her and tried to express what we wanted, something progressive but also traditional," says Campbell.

The describing, however, was not all that easy. Campbell recalls that "the hardest thing was to describe to her what financial planning was all about."

FINDING THE RIGHT NAME

IFP was lucky that its name already fit. Others are not as fortunate. For some financial services companies, corporate identity programs require not only new logos, updated capabilities statements, and new letterhead, but also new names. Before we get more deeply into IFP's graphic make-over, consider the case of Redfield, Brown, Stanger, which had been operating as a fringe benefit planning company for years when Craig Cerretani, Erik Brown, Brian McNally, Ralph Rotman, and Kenneth Stanger decided it was time for a change.

The five principals had all been working in the Boston office of Northwestern Mutual Life Insurance Company and had, according to Craig Cerretani, "kind of sought each other out because we all worked predominantly in the closely held corporate marketplace."

The principals wanted a new name that didn't "connote" a law-firm-type company. "The name change came in a think tank session where we had the five principals get together," recalls Cerretani. "We just threw names out and one of them seemed to stick against the wall.

"We became the Atlantic Benefit Group, Inc., in January 1986. What finally brought us to this name is (a) it's unique, and (b) it's regional.

"This whole corporate identity thing really forced us to focus in on what we do," adds Cerretani. "We didn't want to be perceived as a law firm, financial planning group, or consultants. We are in the insurance business and we want to be perceived as the most objective, most reputable provider of fringe benefits.

"The bottom line is that we're Northwestern people, but we do have our own corporate identity."

FINDING THE RIGHT LOOK

Corporate identity is a growing concern for more and more financial services shops. Big firms like John Hancock, The New England, Travelers, Shearson/American Express, and Paine Webber can afford to spend big bucks on expensive advertising firms that will pull out all the stops and create top-dollar, top-of-the-line corporate identities and campaigns.

But the smaller operation, say the one- to twenty-person shop, typically cannot afford to spend the same kind of money. The alternative is to go with one of the many design firms around the country, firms like Marsha Johnson's Traditions Design Group in Ventura.

Working with Johnson, it didn't take the IFP principals all that long to hit upon the idea of using a lighthouse for the Harbor View Companies' logo—perhaps three or four meetings with the artist. The IFP identity was a different story altogether, taking two to three months from the time they first met Johnson in the fall of 1985.

"The first series of roughs were sort of ordinary." recalls Johnson. "The heart of it wasn't there. It was really frustrating, because [financial planning] is such a broad field. More or less out of desperation I drew from my personal reserve to try to think: Being an ordinary person with no connection to financial planning, what sort of symbol would I respond to?"

What Johnson ultimately designed was a logo that featured two hands forming an oval. In one hand is an ear of wheat; in the other, seeds sown from the wheat.

While Campbell admits the firm's reaction to the IFP logo wasn't as immediate as to the Harbor View lighthouse, they all "bought into it."

"Plant today and you'll reap tomorrow," is the message Campbell sees the logo giving. "The bold lettering of IFP is a change, too. The lettering is tilted, more progressive."

IFP used its new logo on the sign in front of its offices in Ventura as well as in ads in the local press. "The reaction," says Campbell, was "favorable. Most everyone I've seen likes the idea, but I think everyone has a different interpretation of the logo."

"I would say there was a mixture of feelings [about the logo] at first," admits Johnson. "Most of them [at IFP] liked it but had concerns about the emotional appeal."

THE COST OF A
CORPORATE IDENTITY
OVERHAUL

While Johnson says that to design the logo and make it camera ready cost $775, the whole process of corporate identity for IFP, including public relations, design, printing, and advertising, is running them around $20,000 to $23,000, Campbell estimates.

The price for a corporate identity overhaul can range quite widely. For business cards for all principals and sales associates, stationery, envelopes, folders, announcements, and mailing labels, the cost to the Atlantic Benefit Group for design and printing was $5,500, according to Craig Cerretani.

The cost depends on print runs, the amount of time the designer puts in, whether or not any direct mail is being done, and how many different types of pieces will be designed.

THE COMPLEXITY OF
FINDING THE RIGHT LOOK

While IFP was going through an overhaul for the identity of both IFP and the newly created Harbor View Companies, Atlantic Benefit Group had the one name and the one identity to deal with. The fact that their corporate identity needs were limited to the one name didn't make the process any simpler, however.

"The first thing we did was sit down and have some discussion on what they were trying to accomplish," says Bruce Alexander, who owns Aardwolf Advertising in Wilmington, Massachusetts. "How did they want to position themselves?"

"There were some differing opinions," recalls Alexander. "Some at Atlantic Benefit Group wanted a law firm look; some wanted flashy. What we settled on was something contemporary but subtle.

"When you have five principals, it's going to be difficult. Decision by committee doesn't work, especially with something as subjective as design. Craig [Cerretani] and Erik [Brown] eventually handled it; the other guys had power of veto."

The design that Alexander eventually came up with is an embossed periwinkle shell at the center of the letterhead, with six blue horizontal lines beginning near the shell's bottom. The company's name and address are also in blue type.

"Insurance is a very abstract thing as are most financial types of things," says Alexander. "The company principals came up with the name, which I didn't think was bad. I wanted to tie the logo into New England and the coast.

"I was going for something slightly out of the ordinary, but still a conservative look—slightly different, but not radically different. They didn't want to project the image of wild and crazy guys."

TRUSTING THE DESIGN PROFESSIONAL

Building trust between the financial professional and the designer can also take time. "One of the problems," says Alexander, "was I think Craig and Erik realized they were spending a great deal of money with not a lot of control. I think they were uncomfortable at first at spending money and having to trust us. . . . In the insurance business everything is under their control, but in this case they had to trust us."

But "you've hired people who are experts at doing this and you shouldn't tell them what to do," Alexander explains. "You can define your needs; they should be able to meet your needs. I think the transition was when we went from discussions to presentation of ideas, when they started to see visuals and what we could do on paper. They began to trust us more at that point."

"I would say you do your due diligence before you ever meet the design group," says Cerretani. "Know who you are and how you want to be perceived in the marketplace. Once you have the corporate mission and corporate focus, I think the corporate identity is easy to find."

DOES THE NEW LOOK WORK?

One way to judge whether or not a corporate identity is appropriate is whether or not it works. Does it reach the market you're going after? Are you perceived the way you want to be perceived?

Less than two months after a name change announcement went out from the Atlantic Benefit Group with the new corporate identity, they were receiving letters from clients complimenting them on the new look.

Cerretani says he's "convinced that a portion of feedback, a large portion, is a result of the way people perceive us in the marketplace, and I think that comes with the corporate identity. Our philosophy is to be top shelf. Be the best you can be or don't do it at all. That includes your corporate identity."

"It's important that people not look at what I do as art, but as a commercial venture to support their needs," says Alexander. "Whether or not they like it is not as important as whether it works. Of course try to tell the clients that. But it's very conceivable that what [the client] doesn't like [about the logo] is going to work."

Alexander is pleased with the reception of Atlantic Benefit Group's new corporate identity. "I know people have called their office and asked who did the identity program," he says. "That's a point of pride. It also generates more business for us, which is the name of the game."

13 ADVERTISING THAT LIFTS YOU OUT OF THE CROWD

Harry Washburn had his work cut out for him when he approached Weston Financial Group, a Wellesley, Massachusetts, fee-only financial planning firm in 1983. Washburn, a principal in the Cambridge-based marketing consulting group Walsh and Washburn, had been told by a mutual client that Weston could really use some "direction" in their advertising.

"At the outset, they were cautious and rightly so," recalls Washburn. "They had spent more than serious bucks on advertising and had gotten virtually no return on it. They were relatively convinced that advertising wouldn't work. There was no reason for them to think it would have, because no one else in their field at the time was advertising either."

Washburn is an advertising pro. After several years with major advertising firms, including Pearson and MacDonald, Marvin and Leonard, and Humphrey Browning MacDougall in Boston, as well as Benton and Bowles in New York, he struck out on his own.

He's got the charm of the Madison Avenue crowd but the calm of the Cambridge set. He works out of his home on Francis Avenue, just a few doors down from John Kenneth Galbraith's place, around the bend from Julia Child, and down the street from the Divinity School at Harvard. Washburn's an avid jazz fan and saxophone player; he runs a once-a-month "Jazz at Noon" series in Boston.

His client, Weston Financial Group, was formed as a partnership between Rich Horowitz and Doug Biggar at the end of 1978. They incorporated in 1981, at which time they brought on a third partner, Joe Robbat, Jr.

Weston Financial has grown to more than thirty-seven employees, twenty of whom are professional planners. Nine of them hold JD degrees. The client mix is upscale: 50 percent are corporate executives; 25 percent professionals—doctors, lawyers, and college professor types; 25 percent small business owners, manufacturer's reps, and what Horowitz refers to as the "widow-orphan" types who have inherited money. Their clients' minimum income is $100,000.

"Our sense of advertising is that you have to differentiate yourself from everyone else," Horowitz says in his Wellesley office. In two series of ads that Washburn worked with them to develop, Weston Financial Group has done just that.

ADVERTISING THAT'S BOTH INTERESTING AND PROFESSIONAL

The first series of ads is designed to resemble front-page articles in *The Wall Street Journal*. "Upscale people relate to *The Wall Street Journal*," says Horowitz. "It grabs them."

Washburn argues that it's more than the look that grabs them. "It was a real attempt to make it interesting in some way. *The Wall Street Journal* is interesting to read. As an advertising professional, I don't think anything has to be boring. And it certainly doesn't have to be flaky to be interesting. The question is, how do you come up with a piece that is both interesting and professional? We have copy that seems to do it."

"The topics are all pretty conventional topics," Washburn continues. "Are we seeing the last of the limited risk real estate partnerships? Some of the topics are current. Some on tax reform. One on executive compensation, another on tax withholding. All the formats are about the same for the ad. It's a question of finding the right topic and doing it in an interesting way."

Washburn says these ads are "pulling in new clients and also increasingly communicating who Weston is. It's the biggest. It's very professional. I hesitate to say we are 'creating' an image, because Weston already has an image. They continue to develop and get better. My job is to keep up with that and to keep communicating to the public who they are and do it in an interesting manner."

The second series of ads resembles *New Yorker* magazine articles. The one they ran in *Boston* magazine was headlined "This Little Piggie" and had a *New Yorker*–like cartoon of two men, one confiding to the other at a cocktail party, "Pork bellies will never be lower, Bill, it's the chance of a lifetime. And if worse comes to worst, you can always eat your losses."

"When we first saw the pork belly ad," says Horowitz, "Joe and I laughed so hard we were practically in tears."

REAL LEADS AT AN AFFORDABLE COST

Weston Financial runs about one ad a month in *The Boston Globe*, plus one or two a year in *Boston* magazine, depending on whether *Boston* runs a special personal finance section. The ads in the *Globe* (which typically run about 10 column inches) cost $2,500 per ad to run. Washburn estimates that for the two-thirds of a page they buy in *Boston* the cost "is around a grand."

"Our ads are for people who read," says Washburn. "They're editorially oriented ads. And we really deliver some meat in terms of ideas in them."

"In our ads we try to be professional," adds Horowitz. "We don't want to come across like a bank or an insurance company. You really have to separate yourself from the crowd."

When determining how much to spend on advertising, Weston Financial wasn't particularly "scientific" in determining ad/sales ratios. "We looked at how much we projected for income this year," says Horowitz. "Then we just played with the numbers. It wasn't a conscious decision or a percentage. We just said, 'Here's what we want to do in advertising promotions.' Then we saw if it was affordable in the budget."

"Although we do get a good direct response to our ads," says Washburn, "in the long term, you don't try to justify every dollar of advertising expense based on how many new clients are brought in by an ad. I don't think anybody's found a way to exist solely on advertising. We certainly haven't any more than anybody else. If you expect to pay out your ad program dollar for dollar based on new clients brought in, no one has done it yet. You should be getting 50 to 80 percent of new business based on referrals, like any good professional business. I don't think it ever pays out dollar for dollar. If that's what you expect, I think you're barking up the wrong tree. It *should* produce real leads at an affordable cost.

"We looked at how many hours of effort it would have taken to bring in a new client and multiplied it by the cost of these hours. The idea was to shift some of the burden from management to advertising. It's not quite picking a number out of the air.

"Why not take that amount of dough and use it for advertising to see if we can get leads of something in that ballpark? You have to figure half the dough for advertising is going to image, half to get the client."

THE SIDE BENEFITS AND
RISKS OF ADVERTISING

While the approach to advertising that Weston Financial has taken has been innovative, the results have been successful without being overwhelming. "People don't come banging on your doors," Horowitz says. "Out of fifty or sixty responses to the response card in *Boston* magazine last year, we got maybe one new client. I think the cost of the ad will be returned by one new client. But you've also got to ask yourself about all the side benefits you get, like name recognition."

They've found that the *New Yorker*–type ads don't pull as well in the *Globe* as the *Wall Street Journal* ads. Judging from the results of their most recent *New Yorker* ad placement in *Boston*, however, this may be because the *Journal* ad is more appropriate for a newspaper format. Two weeks after the "Little Piggie" ad ran in *Boston*, Weston had already received more than twenty-five response cards.

"Advertising is just so hard," Horowitz says. "You just don't know sometimes. You take chances."

Some clients find Weston's approach to advertising appealing. One client in the advertising business told them the ads "did the trick" when he was trying to decide on a financial planner. On the other hand, when Horowitz was trying to court the business of a major software firm in Cambridge, he was told the ads weren't "professional" enough.

"That's one of the things that our advertising and all aspects of our marketing tells me," muses Horowitz. "I'm convinced Weston is not the answer for all the people we're talking to. If we fail only half the time, it's great."

Horowitz is convinced, however, that risks are worth taking, particularly in marketing his firm. "We tried direct mail and failed horrendously, nothing, a waste. *We* failed, not the direct mail. You try something, think about it, retry it. It can't be a one-shot deal. You monitor it, test it, and be prepared to try it again."

Advertising is a tremendous way for a financial advisory firm to build recognition in the marketplace and even draw in new customers. Advertising is not the answer for all planning firms, however. If a firm is already as large as it wants to be through a referral network, there is obviously no reason to advertise.

The advertising proposition can also bear a large pricetag. First off, there's the cost of producing the ads themselves. Add to this the cost of placing the ads, and you can run up some hefty bills. These costs can be controlled by limiting the variety and frequency of the ads. But then the firm has to determine if a limited number of ads will be effective.

THE COST OF
THE AD AGENCY

The big costs come when an agency or consultant is brought on to work with the firm to develop a solid approach to advertising. "If a firm expects to do it for 5,000 bucks, they can forget it," says Washburn.

"The cost depends on how much you have your ad agency do, but professional fees can range from $25,000 to $50,000 a year, depending on how the agency is structured," says Washburn. "This is certainly for not more than a day a week of an ad executive's time."

Costs may be lower if an agency puts a junior person on the account, but a firm that puts an ad agency or consultant on retainer can expect to pay a minimum of $2,000 a month, plus commissions on ad sales, according to Washburn.

Washburn works on a fee-only basis. "You have to be prepared to invest in the guy," says Horowitz. "You should use the same criteria as you would for shopping for a financial planner. A one- or two-man office like Harry is fine for us. Just like I think there'll always be a place for the one- or two-man financial planning shop. "Harry educated us about advertising. He's expensive, too, but it's a commitment we've made."

Washburn sees his approach as "basically a common-sense approach to advertising. The big challenge is to be interesting without being goofy. Maybe goofy works for somebody, but it wouldn't work in our market. And being boring doesn't work in anybody's market."

14 PUBLIC RELATIONS:
Giving Good Image

In the 1920s, Edward L. Bernays, widely recognized as the father of public relations, had a bacon company as a client. At the time, the typical American's breakfast was a light meal, perhaps toast and coffee. Bernays canvassed several thousand physicians about whether or not a big breakfast was more nutritious than a light meal. The majority of the respondents agreed that a heavy meal, like one consisting of bacon and eggs, just might be the ticket to get the day going in a nutritious way.

Bernays had brought home the bacon to the breakfast table. He had used public relations to influence America's breakfast-eating habits.

While Bernays, whose uncle, by the way, was Sigmund Freud, broke the ground for the building of a new industry, he was not alone in constructing it. Some estimates place the number of public relations firms in this country today near the 10,000 mark. In *O'Dwyer's Directory of Public Relations Executives* for 1986, 1,800 public relations firms chose to be listed. Many of these are small operations, judging from the fact that 1,700 of them bill less than $2 million in fees a year.

WHAT IS PUBLIC RELATIONS?

Just as the number of public relations firms proliferates, so too do the definitions of the profession. Many confuse public relations with publicity or advertising, both of which it is not, at least not precisely, since publicity is one aspect of public relations and some even consider advertising to be part of the overall public relations effort.

Neither is public relations synonymous with marketing. Rather, public relations is one aspect of marketing, along with selling, market research, product development, and other facets of the craft.

On the wall of his Back Bay office in Boston, Matthew Rovner, principal of Rovner Public Relations, has posted a page from the 1985 Boston Ad Club calendar for Monday, November 11, Veteran's Day. Below the date on the page is a quote from Rovner: "Selling Public Relations is like explaining Freedom." So too is defining it.

One of the better, clearer definitions of public relations is used by Lindsay K. Wyatt in her book, *The Financial Planner's*

Guide to Publicity and Promotion (Longman, 1987). Wyatt writes, "Basically when I talk about public relations I talk about concepts of communicating and image. Public relations is a coordinated set of activities designed to communicate your image to your public."

Broad perhaps, but accurate, since the implication is that public relations entails everything that goes into communicating the image you want to communicate to your target audience.

HOW AND WHEN
TO HIRE A PR FIRM

But who needs to hire a public relations firm? How big does your operation have to be before it warrants paying for the services of a public relations professional?

"I think public relations agencies can help firms of all sizes, even individual practitioners," says Wyatt. "It depends on what your needs or objectives are in terms of growth. Public relations should follow your overall business plan. If you're in a situation where you're getting referrals from networking and you don't need new clients, you may not need a public relations firm. But if you want to grow . . . ."

Professionals considering hiring the services of a public relations firm should treat public relations like any other professional service: interview prospective public relations professionals and find out which one can best fill your needs.

Talk directly to the person with whom you will be working. Get a feel about whether or not the prospective practitioner is a person you can work with. If there is any friction or uneasiness about working with a particular professional, no matter how highly he or she comes recommended, think long and hard about whether this is a person you want to work with over a long period of time. "It often takes six to nine months to see any results," says Wyatt. "If you plan to hire a firm and fire them after three months, you might as well give the money to charity."

Once you find a firm or an individual with whom you'd like to work, ask the public relations pro the following seven screening questions:

1. Do you have any similar accounts that might pose a conflict of interest for you?

2. What is your fee structure? Is it retainer plus expenses or on a project-by-project basis? The cost of a public relations campaign will depend on the size of the firm and the size of the particular account. For an independent financial planner, the retainer may range anywhere from $600 to $1,300 per month. Larger firms can expect $3,000 to $5,000.

3. What can you do for me and how will you measure the results? It should not be a mystery. "A good public relations professional should be able to show you measurable results," says Wyatt. "If they say they can't tell if they're doing a good job, you shouldn't be using them."

Some activities, such as seminars where you can track whether attendees are converted to clients, have a built-in response mechanism. Most public relations firms or practitioners will also place a value on any media coverage they get clients.

"Publicity you cannot buy, you cannot guarantee it," warns Rovner. "I evaluate publicity based on its placement in a publication, lineage, and content." To arrive at a dollar figure, Rovner calculates what it would cost to run an ad of similar space in the same publication. He then multiplies that amount by three, figuring in all three variables that add to the publicity's value. "You can't buy the space," says Rovner, "but the client wants to know how to value it."

For example, for an accounting firm he represents, Rovner arranged for interviews with several publications, including one of the Boston dailies, a trade newspaper, a consumer newsletter, and the city magazine. His clients were quoted in each of these publications. Rovner figured that by the end of the fourth month of their relationship, his clients had received in excess of $18,000 worth of publicity just in terms of the amount of lineage, placement, and content. To buy ad space of the same length would have cost more than $6,000, which equaled the first six month's retainer fee.

But the quotes are far better than any ad, says Rovner, because it gives his client "third party credibility." In other words, when people read an article in the newspaper that quotes a professional, it has more credibility than if they read it in an advertisement, since they know the professional can choose to write whatever he or she wants in the advertisement.

To track the overall results of the public relations effort, you should track what happens after you start using public relations even if you cannot directly attribute it to a specific event.

"You should be able to see growth," advises Wyatt. "If you're with a public relations firm for a year and are getting great publicity but not seeing any growth, you shouldn't be spending the money."

4. Who have your clients been? Ask for references. Look for satisfied customers.

5. May I visit your offices? Many public relations firms will offer you full service but in actuality will be contracting out much of the work to free-lancers. While this is not necessarily bad, you should know who is going to do the work, how much it will cost, and whether or not the retainer you might be paying covers any extra freelancers' fees.

If you've hired a large public relations firm rather than an independent practitioner, look for a lot of people and a lot of activity when you visit their office. This doesn't apply if you're hiring a freelancer or an independent.

6. Do you know my business? You should weigh whether you want to pay less and teach someone your business from the ground up, or pay more for someone who already knows your business. Rovner suggests that while it's common to try to find someone who "specializes in your area, a public relations person knows about the public relations business. They can do anything."

7. Who are your press contacts in my field? "One of the things you're looking for is someone who has press contacts," says Wyatt. "Public relations is more than writing a press release," Having the contacts to send a press release to is as important as knowing what to send.

MAPPING OUT A STRATEGY

If you find a public relations professional who can answer your questions satisfactorily, it's then time to sit down with him or her and map out a strategy.

"We make a plan that we come up with the client," explains Rovner. "You sit with the client and you interview him. Find out how he sees his company and how it differs from the rest of the marketplace. We then position the company or individual through ideas or opportunities we can create, something that will stand out to get press attention. We give the press something very newsworthy or very creative for them to respond to."

"We'll interview the client to see where he wants to be," Rovner continues. "Then we'll do some media research, looking for a niche that we can fit into. While we're doing the research, we'll check editorial calendars to see what's coming up." Most magazines will publish an editorial calendar, which is used to let advertisers know when specific matters will be covered in the publication. These calenders are usually available from the magazine's advertising sales representatives.

When he was interviewing his accounting firm client, Rovner found that the principals "wanted people to know they were aggressive and innovative—that they were committed to doing some maverick things, such as financial planning, and that they were in the business of making money off of their brains and not off of other people's products.

"We also found out what types of industries they liked to serve so we could go after publications in those industries, e.g., the building and construction industry, the real estate industry. They also wanted to be known in their area of dominant influence. They wanted to let people know they were around."

With that information in hand, Rovner set out a public relations plan for his client which, through use of his press contacts, resulted in the $18,000-plus worth of publicity.

Had his clients been interested in running seminars on tax reform for small businesses or a Saturday open house for prospective clients, Rovner would have worked with his client to build those public relations events into the overall program.

Had his client wanted to give away a token gift to clients, such as a small booklet on the tax reform with the firm's name printed on it, the effectiveness of that too would have been examined.

Lindsay Wyatt reminds us that public relations "is more than publicity. It's special events, speaking, managing direct mail, coordinating advertising." It's using creative techniques to coordinate the set of activities that ultimately will communicate your image to your public.

Rovner suggests looking at not-so-obvious places to direct public relations efforts. "Firms should think about sponsoring something like 'All Things Considered' on their local National

Public Radio station," he says. "Or perhaps sponsoring something on the local PBS public television station. Those are great places to be heard. You get a lot of good feelings out of that."

Even the obvious, the techniques that have been used for years, often work. On his desk, among a lot of other material, are two NFL-insignia pens embossed with the name *Merle Harmon's Fan Fair*, a chain of retail stores specializing in professional-sports-approved clothings and gifts, which is being syndicated by Financial Equity Group, Inc., of Birmingham, Michigan (see Chapter 4). Inexpensive pens carry the name of the store not only to potential customers but also to potential investors and broker-dealers.

Rovner holds up a calendar, which he received as a gift from a local savings bank. "This is a great idea," he says. "I look at the calendar forty-eight times a day. I may not think of Natick Federal every time, but it's there."

Natick Federal has successfully communicated its image to its public.

15 PRESSING RELATIONS: How to Be a News Source

Andy Warhol once said that in the future everyone will be famous for fifteen minutes. Financial services professionals are queuing up for their share of fame. Business and finance have become glamorous issues, and professionals who are knowledgeable and quotable sources are being sought out by the local and national press.

What are members of the press looking for in sources? How do they find them? Who do they keep going back to for quotes? How can financial services professionals become sources?

The answers vary from writer to writer and advisor to advisor, but there are some key factors that affect whether or not a professional gets coverage.

TELL THEM WHAT YOU KNOW

First and foremost, writers are looking for people who know what they are talking about. Jim Henderson, a personal finance writer with *USA Today* who uses financial advisors as sources in his fortnightly "Your Money Plan," says, "I've made a point of going back to someone if the guy says, 'Look this is really not my area. I'm not well qualified in that subject. I'd love to have my name in the paper, but . . . .' You circle that guy, because you know he's not going to snow you."

Writers are also wary of sources who seem to be pitching only one type of product instead of giving objective advice. "The thing that makes me wary is planners who recommend nothing more than load funds or insurance products," says Andrea Rock, staff writer for *Money* magazine. "I know they're receiving high commissions and not necessarily evaluating it. The planners I would tend to call back and have faith in are those who would recommend no-load *and* load funds.'

BE A RESOURCE, NOT JUST A SOURCE

Laura Waller, a CFP who owns Laura Waller Advisors, Inc., in Tampa, Florida, has been used as a source for *Money*, *USA Today*, and *The Wall Street Journal*, as well as for her local press. She advises that "it's a good idea when the press calls and you can't deal with it to go ahead and give another person's name. Don't fear the competition getting the coverage, because you really become a resource person for the press."

Steven Enright, CFP and director of financial planning at Seidman Financial Services in New York, has been on both sides of the fence. He spent eleven years as a journalist in the newspaper business and, just before becoming a financial planner, was senior financial editor for *Medical Economics* magazine.

"You have to be very careful about pounding your own chest," says Enright. "You cannot take the posture that 'I am the single best source in the world.' If you don't know the subject well, then refer to someone else. The journalist is going to get a better story, and both he and the source [you refer him to] will appreciate it. Everybody wins, even if you're not getting an immediate quote."

In fact, many financial services professionals who find themselves being used regularly as sources for the press are those who are not overzealous about being quoted every time they are interviewed.

Enright, because of his background, is in a unique position to be able to recognize and understand stories that may be of interest to journalists. But he also recognizes the difficulty of a journalist's job.

Enright says, "I have told them all from start, 'You don't *have* to quote me just because you call me.' I've had journalists call me for background *before* they call another planner. Basically you're building a relationship. That's the key with any journalist.

"You have to understand that there are not only occasions when [a journalist] can't quote somebody but also occasions when you [the source] end up on the editing room floor. That's something the financial planner has to understand—sometimes the journalist doesn't have control over his sources getting into his stories."

BE PREPARED AND
SUCCINCT; KNOW THE
DEADLINE

"As a daily writer, there's a pressure for me to look for people who can quickly grasp the thrust of a story, so they can focus their comments," says Jim Henderson. "Usually I outline the story first, what my thesis is, and then go from there. Then pretty much my first question is, 'Am I on target?' I don't need them to belabor all they know. What I'm looking for is something more tangential that they can add to the stories, perhaps anecdotes to illustrate the thing."

"When the press does call me, one of the first things I do is to ask the deadline," says Waller. "I usually do better if I'm not talking off the top of my head."

Henderson's regular sources behave similarly. "I have several sources I've worked with before who say 'Jim, tell me the angle, give me some time, I'll call you back.'"

In fact, it's the unprepared source who often makes the writer's job a nightmare. Alan Lavine, who writes a twice-weekly personal finance column for *The Boston Herald*, finds it difficult to deal with sources who aren't prepared to deal with the press. "They don't think about what they're going to say. I like people who are able to transfer experience very clearly. . . . If they don't know the subject area, they should refer to someone else."

One of the most difficult situations for Lavine and other financial writers to deal with is when a source who doesn't know the topic calls back with an expert in a conference call. The original source still doesn't know anything about the topic, but in his zeal to get quoted, he refuses to refer the writer to the expert without being part of the interview. This makes it difficult for the writer to interview the expert without having the original source take up a lot of time, which is precious to a writer on deadline.

BUILD SOURCES OF REFERRALS

Referrals are one of the ways Lavine and other financial journalists find sources for stories. Writers who find useful sources will also pass source names on to other writers looking for information on similar topics.

Henderson has looked for people who are members of the board of the Institute of Certified Financial Planners (ICFP). "The board of directors of the ICFP have been very good because they understand that part of their duties is to work with the press, so they're cooperative," says Henderson.

Waller is the southern regional director of the board of the ICFP, which is one of the ways she's become known to the press. "It's good for people to serve in different capacities in our professional organizations," she says. "You promote yourself and your profession as well."

For the "Your Money Plan" advisors in *USA Today*, Henderson will use sources he has built a relationship with on other stories. "The money plan takes work," he says. "There's nothing worse than working over a two-week period with someone who is difficult to work with."

DO YOU NEED A PUBLIC RELATIONS FIRM?

Enright realizes that many financial advisors who run small shops "are not in position to hire a public relations firm. There are a lot of planners who get quoted without benefit of a public relations firm. By the time a planner can afford a public relations firm, he probably doesn't need one."

Anthony Katz, senior vice president of Dudley-Anderson-Yutzy, the New York–based public relations arm of the Oglivy & Mather advertising firm, does not agree that financial planners can't afford public relations firms. "You don't have to buy the whole enchilada," says Katz several times during an interview. "What they might get is some counseling or a one-shot project, or perhaps a media plan. They can then implement it themselves."

Henderson feels that the problem for small firms is that they hire public relations people who "don't always know the story they're pitching. The type of PR firm these guys can afford are typically generalists."

LET THE PRESS KNOW YOU'RE THERE

Some planners have managed to make themselves known without the benefit of an outside public relations firm. That does not mean they weren't engaged in public relations efforts.

When Laura Waller moved to Tampa, she started sending out letters of introduction to business editors of the local press.

"I shared my areas of competence and enclosed a resume," she recalls. "Maybe about ten months later the local media did start calling. It was a way of introducing myself in a professional fashion."

Richard Yodites, a financial management advisor with Yodites and Associates in Diamond Bar, California, used a similar method. He sent a letter to *USA Today* identifying his background. They called him and began using him as a source.

Yodites admits that he's gotten no direct business from the mentions in the press, however. "It's a trade-off," he says. "The writer gets some expertise, and I get some very good third party credibility."

"If you know the reporter," says Enright, "I don't think there's anything wrong with calling him up. Unless you know him already, I would not do that. I would put something together on paper, making sure it's to the point. I would follow that up with a phone call a few days later.

"Choosing the people to send information to is important. You don't want to flood the newsroom with press releases. You want to find out who they should go to." Enright recommends consulting *The Editor and Publisher Market Guide*, which lists media business contacts. The yearbook is in the reference room of most major libraries.

What's In the Press Release?

"You want to make sure a press release is directed to the right person, newsworthy, and above all accurate," warns Enright. "Once you lose your credibility with media, it's difficult if not impossible to get it back. The word gets around."

Making a press release newsworthy is important. If you are going to send out a press release, you want to make sure that the information will catch a writer's attention. The whole gist of public relations, according to one PR professional quoted in *America's New Breed of Entrepreneurs* (Acropolis, 1986), "is taking something, even if it's intrinsically boring, and making it fabulously interesting and telling everybody about it."

Local vs. National Press

"When you get local media coverage," says Laura Waller, "you have a lot more clients calling than with national coverage." To make sure her clients know about the national coverage, she sends them clips of articles that may be relevant to their situation.

She always tries to follow up an interview by writing a thank-you note to the writer. "I think that's important," she says. "It certainly helps with public relations."

"All journalists have egos," notes Enright. "Especially if you've been quoted accurately, you might want to drop a written line and thank him for it, nothing too gushing."

INDEPENDENT SOURCES VS. CORPORATE SPOKESPEOPLE

Many journalists will look for independent sources of information rather than people affiliated with large firms. "They've got this big company behind them, but they lack that independence," says Henderson. "Although the head of the financial planning division at a big brokerage firm might be more qualified, he might not be as objective, or unable to talk, or it just might be difficult to get to him. It's tough if you've got to go through the corporate communications department of a big firm when you are on deadline."

Steven Norwitz, vice president in charge of press relations for T. Rowe Price Associates, a firm in Baltimore, Maryland, perhaps best known for its no-load mutual funds, is looked upon by several journalists as one of those corporate communications people who make the interviewing process less painful.

"My background is in journalism," says Norwitz, "so I try to maintain an objective third party perspective of what goes on around here. One of the guidelines I adopted when I started in corporate communications is to step back and ask, 'If I were a reporter, would I find it worthwhile?' If I am not a believer that it's a decent story, I just say forget it.

"I recognize a lot of the pressures journalists are under, so I try to be accessible and get information promptly.

"The number one thing is being honest, particularly in the financial area, where people are not going to invest in you unless they trust you.

"T. Rowe Price is the only corporate communications job I've had. The people here are not gun-shy of talking to the press. They realize for a direct marketing firm like ours that the press is important.

"One of the things I've found is that reporters find a lot of public relations people who are not knowledgeable. I really find that hard to believe. Basically my job is just communicating information in an honest and straightforward way. Fortunately I work for a company that allows me to do that."

Smaller financial planning firms may enjoy the luxury of having corporate communications departments, but Waller advises that it's "important to instruct staff how to put [the press'] calls through, because you're usually dealing with a time thing."

To help members of the press, it's useful to let them know your areas of expertise. "I try to pick people who are specialists," says Henderson, "but that takes some digging."

It's also a mistake to put down your competition. "I would not in any way put down my competition," says Waller. "It reflects poorly on all of us."

Waller also suggests avoiding being "put in the position of giving some slick formula. The public really does take the written word verbatim." For this reason, she advises, "Don't try to bluff. All of us have seen clients take issues and run with them."

To help financial planners deal with the print media, Dudley-Anderson-Yutzy has put together a list of tips you can use. Among their suggestions:

- Don't say anything you wouldn't want to see in print.
- Keep it simple.
- Do not use too many numbers or statistics.
- If you don't know the answer to a question, say so. Offer to get the answer as quickly as possible and do it.
- Always correct the interviewer if a question misstates a fact or is based on an erroneous premise.
- If you promise to get back to the press, do so immediately with the information you promised.
- When near a reporter's deadline, call to inquire if there are any facts you can provide or any information you can cross-check.
- If the coverage was fair, followup with a letter or a note commending the reporter on a good job with a complicated subject.

You may not find yourself on the cover of *People* magazine or profiled on the front page of *The Wall Street Journal*, but in these days when knowledge of personal finance issues is at a premium, you just might find yourself the center of attention for a bevy of financial journalists looking for a source. For financial services professionals, sound knowledge coupled with honesty and the ability to express the issues will better the chances of meeting the press.

16 MAKING NEWSLETTERS PAY: *Publishing Your Own Newsletter*

Creative marketing can make the difference between success and failure for any financial services professional. Two professionals who offer similar services and have fairly similar credentials may have different success stories depending on how they've used public relations, promotions, advertising, or any other aspect of marketing to let prospective clients know they exist. Effective marketing can spell the difference between eking out an existence or flourishing in the trade.

But marketing *can* be costly. Commercial television time for ad spots is not cheap. Radio ads are less expensive but can still take a big bite out the financial pro's budget. Other avenues may prove equally expensive.

Enter the world of innovative marketing. Mike Surratt, a financial advisor and registered representative with J. H. Shoemaker and Company in Memphis, Tennessee, may have figured out a way to use a traditionally expensive marketing tool and ultimately have it pay for itself.

IDENTIFYING THE NEWSLETTER MARKET

The marketing tool is a monthly eight-page client newsletter called *Mid-South Investor*. Started more than four years ago by Surratt, the newsletter is sent free every month to the 2,500-plus active clients of the fifteen advisors at Shoemaker and Company, which is an affiliate of the Atlanta-based Financial Service Corporation (FSC).

"The newsletter is also sent to a computerized list that rotates out 13,000 names and addresses," says Surratt, who is the newsletter's managing editor. "The computer system rotates those names. If someone received one . . . and is not a client, he might only get it quarterly. But clients with any one of the fifteen of us are put on the computer system and receive it monthly."

Roughly 4,500 people receive the newsletter each month. Surratt estimates a readership of 10,000 by the time the issues are routed through offices.

The newsletter is not too different from many newsletters offering financial planning advice to planners' clients. Every month there's a variety of articles ranging from refinancing your home to using market timing strategies. Sometimes the articles are by Surratt; other times Shoemaker or other advisors at the firm will contribute an article.

What makes *Mid-South Investor* different from many of the client newsletters out there is that Surratt sells advertising space. What's more, he expects that that advertising will pay for the total cost of the newsletter—everything from production to printing to postage—within a year. "Advertising may pay for 25 percent of it now," says Surratt. "The other 75 percent comes out of our pockets."

He adds, "The cost for *Mid-South Investor* in its present state with postage runs about 50 cents a copy. Postage ranges from a low of around 10.01 cents to a high of 12.2 or 12.3 cents." Surratt explains that they have "clients in something like twenty-two or twenty-three different states among the fifteen of us here," which accounts for the variance in postage rates. The majority of Surratt's clients are in Tennessee, Mississippi, Arkansas, and the "boothill of Missouri," which is the southern part of the state.

The inner four pages of the newsletter are made up of advertisements. A paid full-page ad runs around $250 to $300.

Surratt will run unpaid ads in the newsletter if there is client interest in a particular type of product. In a recent issue, a full-page ad was run for Kagin's Numismatics, Inc., an ad for which Kagin's did not pay. "The Kagin's arrangement was that we had a lot of inquiries about rare coins and numismatics," says Surratt. "We're not locked into any one firm, but we needed someone with a camera ready picture of rare coins, and Kagin's had it."

When there's client interest in particular areas, Surratt can choose from a variety of ads to run in the newsletter. "I have a folder probably 12 inches thick that has virtually every ad mat every mutual fund company has," he says. On the bottom of the ads a coupon is attached for the reader to send in for more information. Surratt's name and phone number are at the bottom of most of the ads.

Paid ads for the newsletter have come from companies ranging from Keystone Mutual Funds to Angeles Corporation, an investment management firm.

USING CABLE TV TO
ATTRACT NEWSLETTER
ADVERTISERS

Paid ads have not been as forthcoming as those Surratt decides to run gratis. But, largely because of Surratt's foray into cable television, that is beginning to change.

In November 1985, Surratt began taping a cable television show that began running at the end of that month. The show is called "Mid-South Investor." Surratt is the host and producer of the show. He will not discuss the costs involved, short of saying "costs are involved on both sides." Surratt and Cablevision, the cable company running the show, are sharing the costs.

On each show, Surratt hosts a panel of experts on a particular issue—experts who are prime targets as potential advertisers in this newsletter.

"It's a lot easier [to get an ad] after someone is a guest panelist," says Surratt. "We always get around to asking if they are interested in placing an ad in the newsletter. We probably have a 70 to 80 percent response rate. It's not that much money for them."

Surratt has completed taping thirty-two shows. The same show is repeated five times a week on Cablevision in the Tennessee market. The guests on the show may be brokers, financial planners, attorneys, accountants, or other financial services professionals. Their company affiliation is never announced on the show.

"You have liability situations," explains Surratt. "I can't have a person coming in selling a product. The program will always be generic and educational," a situation, Surratt explains, that results from both his preferences and his contract with Cablevision.

"I get a great deal of help from FSC's compliance department in all marketing efforts—the television show and the newsletter," says Surratt. "They keep us compliant with all NASD [National Association of Security Dealers] and SEC [Securities and Exchange Commission] requirements."

Surratt wants the state educational television systems in Tennessee, Arkansas, and Mississippi to pick up "Mid-South Investor." And, never one to miss a potential marketing opportunity, he's talking to area radio stations about running the audio portion of the show.

DEVOTING TIME TO MARKETING

All of this marketing takes time—time that could be spent selling product. But Surratt is sold on marketing. "I personally believe an independent financial advisor or planner should include 20 to 25 percent of his professional time in marketing and public relations," he says.

"There is no one else in the mid-South that has a television series. Because of the marketing exposure from this alone, I'm being asked to speak to different groups, and different companies have me in to speak to their executives. A lot of goodwill is created with product sponsors.

"I would say the marketing effort is translating into an increase in the top end of my business, the extremely large accounts. I don't know that the comptroller of a company is not watching the show. He may see something he likes and schedule me to speak to management about personal financial planning. Those are ideal opportunities that probably wouldn't come along if it weren't for the newsletter and television show.

"We as independent financial advisors who belong to independent broker-dealers do not have multimillion ad budgets behind us. We have to compete in this marketplace. Instead of trying to compete head-on with major firms, I try to find out what information individuals want to know and help them with personal finance.

"I think to place an ad in the newspaper or hold seminars may work for some. But it's not the way I want to go, because as far as I am concerned I become another member of the pack. I try to differentiate myself.

"It's very time-consuming, but competition is so great now that financial planners who do not pay attention to public relations, marketing, advertising, and promotion may be left short."

17 IMPRINT NEWSLETTERS:
Imprint We Trust, All Others Pay Cash

Consider Claire Longden. Every other month she sends an eight-page newsletter to her eighty or so active clients along with a personal memo about the economy and the investment markets. The newsletter has articles about topics ranging from futures contracts and international stocks to mutual fund investments and strategies for saving for a college education.

Were Longden to prepare the newsletter herself and turn to a local print shop that would agree to do such a short-run print job, it would cost her $600 to $800 for typesetting alone and another $300 to $350 to print up 100 copies. That's $9.00 to $11.50 per issue, and it doesn't include the cost of envelopes and postage or the time to research, write, and edit the publication.

"One lady thought I wrote it all," laughs Longden, CFP, who is first vice president for Butcher and Singer in Manhattan. "I don't have time."

Instead, Longden turned to Liberty Publishing in Danvers, Massachusetts, one of the growing number of imprint newsletter publishers—publishers that sell preprinted newsletters and envelopes to professionals with the professionals' logos emblazoned across the masthead of the publication.

Longden buys 100 copies of Liberty Publishing's *The Financial Insider*, that company's flagship publication, begun in 1981. For that she pays, in addition to the one-time setup charge of $30 that every new customer pays, 80 cents per issue, a price that includes 9×12 mailing envelopes imprinted with her logo plus all the costs involved in the labor of researching, writing, editing, pasting up, and printing the newsletter. She saves more than 90 percent by not doing the newsletter herself.

CHOOSING THE RIGHT PROVIDER

Liberty is not even the cheapest provider of imprint newsletters. (See the listing at the end of this chapter for a comparison of per-unit costs on orders of 100 newsletters at various imprint houses.)

For example, on orders of 100 copies, prices range from 20.4 cents per issue and a $12 setup fee for Longman Financial Services' four-page *Creative Financial Planning* on up. Prices drop significantly if orders total more than 100. On 500 or more of *Planning Ahead: A Monthly Review of Financial News and Ideas*, a four-page newsletter put out by Atrium Publishing Company in Manhasset, New York, the per-issue price drops all the way down to 17.7 cents, plus a one-time set-up price of $17.50.

The answer to how these imprint publishers provide such savings is obviously volume. They print thousands of these newsletters a month, and not only is their fixed typesetting cost spread over a greater number of issues, their printing costs drop dramatically on large press runs.

"We send out about 150,000 issues a month," says Mark J. Rosen, chartered financial consultant (ChFC), president of Liberty Publishing. "Making it economically feasible is important, so in September 1986 we set up our own print shop."

Among the major providers of imprint newsletters, Liberty is the only one in the financial planning market that prints its own newsletter in-house on company-owned presses rather than sending it out to be printed.

SUBTLE MARKETING TOOL

"The cost of doing a newsletter on your own is certainly higher," Rosen says. "The first thing the planner has to do is to write, edit, and research the facts. Second, he has to go out and find vendors to set type or type it himself, and then it's got to be printed. To get high quality with small print jobs, you generally can't get it done by quick-print shops. It gets to be expensive. A person would certainly spend a lot more money and time doing it on his own. The convenience of having accurate, well-documented material delivered in a package is well worth it. To spend around $80 a month to keep clients informed, there's no more effective way of communicating with the professional community or clients or prospects.

"It's a subtle marketing tool. It keeps the name of the financial planner in front of his client. Very few financial planners have budgets. Those that budget at all don't have a budget for marketing. Here's a low-cost way of marketing for the financial planner."

THE TRADE-OFFS: PERSONAL VS. COMMERCIAL NEWSLETTERS

But what are the trade-offs? Can a newsletter prepared by another provider give a professional's clients the type of information they need for their particular financial or lifestyle situations?

"It's more cost-effective to buy a commercial letter than to sit and do it yourself," says Julius Donner, chartered life underwriter (CLU), and founder of Atrium Publishing, "but it cannot have the same personal tone as a custom letter related to a customer's own situation. I recommend people do certain things, such as every once in a while when they see relevant articles to clip and send them. Write a cover letter every once in a while."

For many financial services professionals, sacrificing customization is more than made up for by the single most important attribute cited for these imprint newsletters: they keep your name in front of the client every month, or every other month, depending on how often you send them out.

"It's a reminder that we think of our clients every month," says Carl Kaliszewski, a financial planner with The Network in Worcester, Massachusetts, who has been using Longman's four-page monthly *Creative Financial Planning* for about two years. "It's good for public relations and advertising and leads to additional business. I send out 200 copies a month and pay for it myself. I doubt I could do it more cheaply. It runs me about $40 a month."

GETTING READER RESPONSE

Most of the imprint newsletter publishers also sell reader response cards that are imprinted with the professional's logo. These can be enclosed with the newsletter, and customers can check off if they want more information on a particular topic. Also provided on these preprinted, postage-paid reply cards is an area where the customer can list others who might be interested in the professional's services, which works as a referral mechanism of sorts.

Like the newsletters, the response cards range in price, from 6 cents each for orders of 12,001 or more at Liberty to 21.9 cents each for orders of 500 or more at Atrium. Longman doesn't sell reader response cards for its newsletters, but that has not stopped some Longman newsletter users from developing their own response mechanism.

"I designed a postage-paid reply card that cost me maybe 3 cents a card," says Longman user Carl Kaliszewski. "It's a simple card saying 'Send me information on the following items—mutual funds, tax-free investments,' and so on."

POSTAGE COSTS

Postage costs become another factor that drives up the cost of any newsletter. For small mailings, the cost of a bulk-rate permit, which drops the 22-cent per-issue price to 18 cents, is not profitable on an annual basis until the size of the mailing reaches around 225.

Take it from Earl Miller, a registered representative with Waddell and Reed in Elgin, Illinois, who has been using Reston Publishing Company's *The Financial Independence Letter* for about a year. "I'm using first-class postage," he reports, "because it's not feasible to use bulk rate yet. I need to be sending out 222 issues a month to reach break-even for the $100 bulk-rate permit. Then I'll go to 18 cents postage. Since I'm sending out 200 copies now, I will have to think about going to bulk rate soon."

Once the decision is made to go with a bulk-rate mailing, the imprint houses will print the bulk-rate permit on the envelopes you buy from them.

EVALUATING
NEWSLETTER CONTENT

Another serious concern for financial services professionals who are considering sending a newsletter to their clients is the content of the letter. Is it product oriented? Is it too technical? Is it too simplistic? Is it written well? Does it address the needs and concerns of their client base?

The only way for planners to determine if any of the

newsletters are appropriate for their clients is to read some sample issues of the newsletters available and determine for themselves. Ask any two planners who use the same imprint newsletter and you're likely to get one who thinks the material is simplistic, another who thinks it's too complex.

"In the financial planning business, it is important to have the right copy," says Liberty president Mark Rosen, who earned his ChFC in 1979 and worked as a financial planner until he decided in the 1980's to devote his full attention to Liberty Publishing. "One thing I feel good about with our newsletter is that you get information. We write about oil and gold, and the economy. Everyone else dances around it. We've got the background and have an understanding of what they want and give it to them."

When Rosen says "we" he really means "I," since it is his words that appear in all the Liberty Publishing newsletters. He reads the monthly copy into a cassette recorder, a secretary transcribes his words, and he edits and reshapes the articles to his satisfaction. Rosen is the only owner/publisher of an imprint newsletter house who writes his own copy.

The average article in a Liberty newsletter runs ten to fifteen paragraphs. They run slightly longer in Longman's newsletters, slightly shorter in Atrium's and Reston's.

"Because I'm a financial planner and have been for many years," says Rosen, "I take this as a personal thing. Clients are the lifeblood of my business. Everything I write is geared to clients."

What the clients are provided with in these newsletters would generally bring joy to the Joe Friday in all of us—the facts, just the facts. Little interpretation is added to the discussion of investment vehicles and tax issues, and when it is added, it's pretty obvious stuff. But it's for this reason precisely that many users like the content.

Says Claire Longden, user of Liberty's *The Financial Insider*, "It has good, basic information on subjects, not too simple, but good background information. When I've looked at others, they've seemed too detailed. Liberty will talk about using convertible bonds, for example, but they won't say whether or not to use them, just *how* to use them. Their newsletters are directed to a planning client, so it's more appropriate than what the client gets from the newspapers, if [he or she] ever gets around to reading the newspaper."

Frank Nelsen, who sells insurance in Sterling, Illinois, with Wilkins-Lowe and Company, uses Longman's *Your Personal Financial Planning* as a prospecting tool to send to qualified leads. "I like it because it's short and not too cumbersome," says Nelsen. "Other newsletters have too much information, which can be over the clients' heads. [You're not always] dealing with super-sophisticated clientele."

FACTORS TO CONSIDER IN CHOOSING AN IMPRINT COMPANY

For some who have decided to use an imprint newsletter publisher, the decision about which one to use is easier than for others. Says Earl Miller, who uses Reston's *Financial Independence Letter*, "The Reston newsletter is the only one we are authorized to send out through Waddell and Reed."

For others whose decisions are not so fixed, decisions such as content, service, price, and quality of design and production will play a crucial role in deciding which product to use. By far the most sophisticated operation appears to be Liberty Publishing, the only firm to actually print its own newsletters. Because it does its own printing, and because Rosen has established an elaborate computerized control system in which every user receives a numbered code that appears on all items ordered, he is the best equipped to handle any last-minute crises that may occur.

Longman, which before it acquired R and R Newkirk's *Your Personal Financial Planning* and *Tax and Financial Report* was marketing its own *Creative Financial Planning*, has recently begun to market its newsletters more aggressively. But it has not gotten the bugs out of its systems yet.

"In July [1987] they missed sending us a shipment," says Carl Kaliszewski. "They cleared that up rapidly and credited us on a future bill. That was the best thing as far as I was concerned, because to send out at the end of July was worthless."

But Longman users too sing its praises for responsiveness to crises. Gloria Foote, a registered representative with First Liberty Securities in Carlsbad, California, uses *Your Personal Financial Planning*. "Longman has been very good," she says.

"I had a question about an article and they researched it for me. I had problems with the glue on their envelope and within 24 hours I had new envelopes."

If glossy versus nonglossy stock makes a difference to you, Liberty is the only imprint publisher to publish all of its newsletters on a glossy stock. The others, with the exception of Longman's *Creative Financial Planning*, are published on an uncoated stock. But while a glossy stock is more expensive, it too is a matter of taste.

"We're primarily two things," says Liberty's Mark Rosen, "a marketing tool for the financial planner and a forum for educating the client, and I guess a third thing, as well," he adds. "We get letters from financial planners saying, 'Gee, I didn't know that.' Our newsletters were never designed to educate the financial planner, but I am getting that response."

"I think it's worth the money," says Frank Nelsen. "First of all, it keeps our name in front of the customer on a monthly basis, but it also establishes more respect, more diversification, and makes more financial tools available in our office. We thought about doing our own newsletter, but the savings we're facing [using an imprint publisher] are incredible."

"Besides," says John Syverson, ChFC, a financial planner with Chartered Financial Services Limited in Des Moines, Iowa, who has been using Longman's *Creative Financial Planning* for about four years, "We're in the financial planning business, not in the newsletter business."

COMPARISON SHOPPING FOR IMPRINT NEWSLETTERS: AVERAGE UNIT COST ON ORDERS OF 100 COPIES

ATRIUM PUBLISHING
1615 Northern Boulevard
Manhasset, NY 11030
516-365-7144

Planning Ahead: 4 pages monthly
29.5 cents per copy, $17.50 one-time setup charge
Contents: short articles on insurance, retirement, estate planning

The Financial Consultant: 4 pages, bimonthly
39 cents per copy, $17.50 one-time setup charge
Contents: short, very basic articles on tax planning, retirement planning, estate planning, and life insurance

Family Finance: 4 pages, bimonthly
39 cents per copy, $17.50 one-time setup charge
Contents: short, very basic articles on estate planning, tax planning, education planning, and insurance

Business Incorporated: 4 pages, bimonthly
39 cents per copy, $17.50 one-time setup charge
Contents: short, very basic articles on tax, financial, and estate planning for corporate business owners

LIBERTY PUBLISHING, INC.
199 Newbury St., Suite 118
Danvers, MA 01923
617-777-5000
800-722-7270

The Financial Insider: 8 pages, monthly
80 cents per copy, $30 one-time setup charge
Contents: geared specifically to a financial planning market; articles range from investment options, estate planning, explanations of economic indicators, tax planning, and retirement to a broad range of planning issues.

Net Equity: 4 pages, bimonthly
58 cents per copy, $30 one-time setup charge
Contents: shorter articles on financial planning issues such as the impact of inflation on investments, tax reform, how to calculate the alternative minimum tax, and how to borrow from a pension plan

Financial Statements: 4 pages, monthly
$1.15 per copy, $30 one-time setup charge (sold only as a package that includes newsletter, envelope, and reader response card)
Contents: three- or four-paragraph articles that focus on personal finance and how economy will affect personal finances; a third of the back page reserved for the user to print a one-paragraph message (such as information about his or her company), which can be changed quarterly.

LONGMAN FINANCIAL SERVICES PUBLISHING
520 North Dearborn Street
Chicago, IL 60610
800-428-3846
800-654-8596 (in IL)

Creative Financial Planning: 4 pages, monthly
20.4 cents per copy, $12 charge for each change in imprint
Contents: fairly long (for a newsletter) articles on estate planning, tax planning, and investment planning; while basic, presents good strategies for the novice investor and financial planning client.

Your Personal Financial Planning: 4 pages, monthly
40 cents per copy, $12 charge for each change in imprint
Contents: a little less flair in design than *Creative Financial Planning*, with similar articles on budgeting, spending, saving, and investing

Tax and Financial Report: 4 pages, monthly
40 cents per copy, $12 charge for each change in imprint
Contents: more technical than other Longman newsletters but still basic; articles on everything from PIGs (passive income generators) to QTIPs (qualified terminable interest property) trusts and borrowing from a retirement plan

RESTON FINANCIAL PUBLISHING, INC.
1850 Centennial Park Drive, Suite 300
Reston, VA 22091
703-860-8400

The Financial Independence Letter: 4 pages, monthly
41 cents per copy, $30 one-time setup charge
Contents: brief, basic, but cogent articles on the economy, tax planning, investment planning, insurance planning, and other topics related to financial planning.

18 LATCH-ON ADVERTISING: *The John Hancock Campaign*

A new type of advertising thrust brings with it a plum opportunity for the country's many small financial advisory shops. A number of major financial services firms have launched ad campaigns depicting the need for some type of financial planning. Many of these companies do not provide the same personal financial planning services provided by independent advisors, but rather sell products.

While the small financial advisory shop can't afford the kind of national marketing campaign a major financial services firm can undertake, it can capitalize on the growing public awareness of financial planning such campaigns are designed to foster and tap into an already receptive market.

THE "REAL LIFE" CAMPAIGN

Perhaps the best example of ads that present latch-on marketing potential has been seen in the "Real Life/Real Answers" campaign John Hancock rolled out in December 1985. These ads have been hard to avoid, even for those with no interest in financial planning.

A visual comes onto the screen: "Michael Mark, Single, Age: 26." The print is white on a black screen. The frame then switches to Michael himself, sitting in a kitchen with his older brother, Dave, who asks him, "So how much you making now?"

"I'm doing fine," Michael responds.

Not satisfied, Dave pursues, "You got to be making at least twenty-five."

"I'm fine," Mike assures him. "Maybe a little better than that," he adds, clearly not one to undercut his own earning ability.

"Thirty? Tell me, yes or no, are you making thirty?" Dave pushes on while most of the home audience wonders why Mike is putting up with such a brazen display of forwardness. Then again, the writer may have dreamed up the aggressive, almost obnoxious Dave while contemplating the ad's audience—college bowl football fans.

"Yes," Mike says.

The ad cuts back and forth between a black-and-white printout of Mike's estimated expenses and the kitchen scene. When Mike admits to making $30,000, that figure flashes on the screen along with his needs: "to limit tax liability to build investments."

But Dave won't let up yet. "You got any investments, any stuff?" he asks.

"Got the car," says Mike.

"That's not an investment. You got an IRA, life insurance?"

"No, not really," Mike, who must be feeling like a total idiot for thinking his car was an investment, admits.

"You're making thirty and you don't have anything like that? What d'ya think? You're eighteen years old or something?"

It's not until after this final brotherly chiding that we get the first indication of who is running these ads. The screen goes black. On it is printed in white, "Answers." The answers, all products, are "John Hancock IRAs, John Hancock Variable Life, John Hancock Mutual Funds."

If you haven't met Michael Mark, the single salesman, perhaps you do recall Margaret and Tom Fitzgerald, the childless married couple in their early thirties waiting to close on a house; or Bill Heater, the thirty-year-old father of two who makes $35,000 a year and wants to protect the long-term needs of his family, one of whom is a six-month-old infant he cuddles in his arms; or maybe you saw a teary-eyed Irving Marcelle, a thirty-seven-year-old retiring football player seeking a "stable transition to retirement."

The ads have been lauded by both the public and the advertising industry. The brainchild of Hill, Holliday, Connors, Cosmopulos, Inc., John Hancock's Boston-based advertising firm, the ad campaign was budgeted at $20 million for 1986. Since their initial rollout, the ads have garnered virtually every award imaginable—among others, the Clio, the Andy, and the prestigious 1986 Grand Prix from the Cannes International Film Festival for the best overall ad. (Only two other United States firms had won the coveted Grand Prix since 1979— BBDO [Batten, Barton, Durstine & Osborn] in 1985 for its Pepsi-Cola "Archaeology" ad and Chiat/Day in 1984 for its Apple Computer "1984" ad.)

The John Hancock ads ran during every major college bowl game on all the major networks in December 1985 and January 1986 and then again during the professional football play-offs and Super Bowl XX before they began to run regularly. In case you missed the television spots, you probably ran into the print ads that began running in January 1986 in *Newsweek, Time, Sports Illustrated, People, Money, Sylvia Porter's Personal Finance Magazine, Changing Times,* and *Smithsonian.*

The ads were ubiquitous. And because of their personal finance bent, talk of them buzzed among players in the financial services industry. Interestingly, while the ads harped on the need for planning, the intent of the ads was not to offer complete personal financial planning but rather to reposition John Hancock as a complete financial services company instead of simply another insurance company.

This intent is one of the reasons that the John Hancock signature does not appear until the very end of the ad. The ad agency did not want to lose viewers immediately by having them think, "Oh, another insurance ad." By having the vignette first and making it appear to be a real-life situation, the ad's writers hoped to intrigue the audience with situations perhaps near and dear to them. In fact, the vignettes are fictional, except for the fact that Oakland Raider Tony King portrays Irving Marcelle in the retiring football player ad and Bill Heater, who wrote the pieces for Hill, Holliday, appears with his real-life daughter in the Bill Heater spots. When the Hancock name flashes on the screen, it does so with the tag *financial services,* not life insurance.

While the ads portray the need for planning, the solutions offered to the real-life problems are all product oriented. John Hancock Financial Services is in the product business, not the financial planning business—at least not yet.

WHOM DO THE ADS HIT?

But, at a time when the International Association for Financial Planning (IAFP) has pumped millions of dollars into a public awareness campaign, can the Hancock ads add to the public's perception of a need for more than auto insurance, a bond mutual fund, Tucker Anthony Securities, an IRA, or other John Hancock–provided financial products?

"I believe that any kind of positive exposure that the general public receives is good," says Beverly Tanner, CFP, with Planned Investments, Inc., in Larkspur, California. "If it can move one or two people to do something they wouldn't ordinarily have done, then I think it's very good."

John Hancock executives boast that the ads have been successful in achieving what they were designed to do—change the public perception that Hancock only sells insurance. "The big objective was to convince people we were more than an insurance company," says Dave D'Alessandro, senior vice president of corporate communications at John Hancock. "We've had a tremendous leap in image statistics."

By late July 1986, D'Alessandro reported, "the image of the company as being diversified had tripled. [Hancock] business is running 15 to 20 percent ahead of competition. It's not all because of advertising, but the advertising certainly can't be counted out as a contribution."

But changing the image has not been the only thing the ads have helped. "The advertisting has also helped us attract a more qualified agent," says D'Alessandro. "Instead of getting ten applications for a job opening, we're getting more than a hundred."

Not everyone agrees, however, that the ad campaign was all that successful in repositioning John Hancock. "I think people still associate John Hancock with insurance," says Charles B. Lefkowitz, CFP, with Financial Blueprints, Inc., in Florham Park, New Jersey. "The solution is always one of their products, and I think people see right through it. I don't think they're hitting my market, but I would guess they are hitting the $20,000 to $60,000 or lower-middle market."

This, according to Herb Gold, John Hancock's senior vice president of sales, is exactly the market John Hancock was going after. "I think we were trying to give the impression that there was not a great need for sophisticated financial planning for the broad range of middle America. We have identified that middle America and want to heighten their awareness to provide products.

"The vignettes really were not sophisticated financial plans. They really identify simple needs, very identifiable needs. Our strength is with mainstream America, and that's really where the ad campaign was directing itself." Gold adds that he can't remember a better sales year in the twenty-five he's been with the company than the year they began the ads.

According to Gold and D'Alessandro, while John Hancock is "testing" pilot programs in financial planning, the company currently does not offer it as a service. "We are developing the technology to determine needs and solve needs," says Gold. He says Hancock's financial planning "package will not be based on product sales. We will be developing the pilot program. It will take us over the next twelve to eighteen months to debug various mechanical things experienced with the pilots. I'd say it would be a two-year rollout."

THE EFFECT ON THE
OVERALL FINANCIAL
SERVICES COMMUNITY

"My attitude is very positive," says one Massachusetts financial advisor. "They deal with issues that are typically bandied about in a very euphemistic way. Hancock has identified itself as a financial services company. It has broadened [the public's] understanding. What bothers me about the ads is that they don't indicate solutions other than products. There's much more to the solution than the product only. They're not making solutions that are planning oriented, but rather product oriented.

"All it does is increase the public's awareness that it should go to a professional. It increases the public's awareness that planning is necessary. But does a person then choose a planner or a product person?"

This advisor says that while he may not be getting calls specifically from people who have seen the Hancock ads, "more and more I'm getting cold calls. As a whole, the public is becoming more aware of planners. I've had a larger response to the IAFP public awareness campaign and the ICFP than any other ad." The Institute of Certified Financial Planners (ICFP) runs a co-op print ad on which CFPs can pay to be listed.

This advisor, like others, believes that the public is more aware now of what financial planning is and of its necessity. "I get referrals from two main sources," he says. "One is from satisfied customers; the other is from the Yellow Pages or people who have seen my name. Unquestionably, people are more aware now of what financial planning is and what the Registry [of Financial Planning Practitioners] is. People now interview me like they're interviewing an attorney. I also don't have to do as much explaining of what financial planning is."

At first, the advisor recalls, he thought the television advertising done by major financial services companies would have a devastating effect on the independent financial advisor.

"I thought, 'Oh my God, they're going to take my business.' Every time one of those companies began an ad campaign, I was convinced that they were going to get the client."

But that has changed. "I'm not afraid of what someplace like Hancock is going to do, because it raises public awareness. Besides, people *do* realize that they may get more attention from a smaller company than a behemoth organization."

The task for Hancock is to create a perception of needs in the public and let the public know that Hancock just might be the financial services company that can fill their needs. If this awareness is created effectively enough, both Hancock and the independent financial advisor can benefit, particularly if the advisor can latch on to the awareness created by the multimillion-dollar marketing efforts of the major financial services firms.

"The more people are aware," says D'Alessandro, "the more they'll get some needs met."

PART FIVE
SELLING
THE GOODS

In every professional practice, there comes a time when theory has to be laid aside and good old-fashioned selling takes hold. Were it not for the sale, the practice would be merely a pipe dream.

Finding the right price for professional services rendered is an issue wrestled with by the rookie and the veteran financial services professional. In Chapter 19, a variety of practitioners and experts provide formulas and innovative ideas for effectively pricing your services.

From his offices in Boca Raton, Florida, Jim Barry has perfected the art of the sales pitch. In Chapter 20, you'll see how he compliments his clients on their professional prowess, then tells him they need someone with equal prowess to manage their money. The man talks fast, makes sense, sells a bundle of mutual funds, and establishes an empathy with his client base that is hard to match.

Over the last several years, Dr. Kerry L. Johnson has earned the moniker of the "sales psychologist." Traveling around the country, Johnson teaches his audiences how to use psychological techniques to sell. In Chapter 21, he details what he calls "subliminal selling skills," which give the professional the tools to match their prospects' primary mode of expression and win them over. Not manipulate, mind you. But rather, win them over by giving them what they want. Johnson explores the techniques of neurolinguistic programming, with an added bit of finesse to train his audiences to close sales and build a satisfied customer base.

Lighten up. That's precisely the function of "corporate training relief films" like the Muppet Meeting Films, which are profiled in Chapter 22. Used as light touches in intensive training or sales meetings, Muppet Meeting Films give the professionals a chance to relax, to reflect on what they've learned, and then to take their marketing and sales knowledge out and knock 'em dead in the marketplace.

Using seminars to build a client base has been tried by many financial services professionals. Few have made it into a profitable venture. Enter Vern Hayden, who has mastered the science of seminars to increase his sales. In Chapter 23, Hayden lays out how to run and track the results of a seminar successfully, down to the last detail.

19 HOW MUCH DOES IT COST? I'LL BUY IT: *Pricing Advisory Services*

In the summer of 1986, Joan R. Powers, CFP, who owns Powers Financial Planning, Inc., in Austin, Texas, was visiting Boston. As most visitors to Boston are wont to do, she picked up a copy of *Boston*, the city's magazine, to get an idea what was going on in town. In the issue, she happened upon an interview with Carol Nathan, a member of the Registry of Financial Planning Practitioners, who is also president of the greater Boston chapter of the International Association of Financial Planning (IAFP).

Powers is a fee-only planner in Austin, a city that has been hit with the same economic malaise that has hit many Texas cities of late. In addition to her work as a financial planner, Powers is an enrolled agent who can practice tax preparation before the IRS, so the income from that work has helped to keep cash coming into the firm, which has one other employee—a paraplanner—and services somewhere between forty and fifty clients. Earlier in the year, she had also raised her hourly rate from $60 to $75, which helped increase cash flow.

FIRST-HOUR CONSULTATION DISCOUNT

But when she read the interview with Nathan, Powers discovered another pricing strategy that would help cash flow. In the interview, Nathan, a fee-plus-commission planner whose income is 90 percent derived from fees, noted that while some planners charge nothing for the first hour of planning, she charged for the first hour of financial planning at a discounted rate.

"I had originally been offering a free first hour," says Powers. "I was realizing that some people were just coming in looking for a few hours. When I read the article in *Boston* magazine about that woman who was discounting the first hour, I decided to try it."

With a regular hourly fee of $75, she offered the initial hour for $50. "Charging the initial fee worked very well," she says. "The number of people coming in hasn't stopped at all. [Considering that] Austin is quite depressed at the moment, we're holding up remarkably well."

DETERMINING A PRICE
STRUCTURE

Pricing of services is an issue that hits all fee-only and fee-plus-commission financial advisors. How can I price my services to make sure that my business is profitable?

"The way I work is when somebody calls, I do a quick interview on the phone," explains Nathan, whose MetroWest Financial Corporation is based in Framingham, Massachusetts. If the person decides he or she needs financial planning, "we set a date. We send out a personal financial survey, which he completes and mails in or brings with him. At the first meeting we go over the survey and identify concerns and financial issues which need to be addressed.

"For that first meeting, I charge a reduced hourly rate of $55 for the first hour as opposed to a normal hourly rate of $85. I tell them the rate up front."

Nathan explains that the reason she doesn't give the client the first hour free is that "I found that I was frequently giving financial planning advice right from the beginning. Occasionally, I even ran into a client for whom 1.5 hours would take care of his problem."

If that's the case, why charge a discounted rate?

"The reason for the reduced rate is that a large portion of our first meeting is dedicated to just getting to know each other. As a result, they are not getting 100 percent of my brain power, my financial expertise."

There is no one answer to how financial planners should price their services. Some planners will offer the first hour of planning free; others will charge. Still others, like Nathan and Powers, will offer the first hour at a reduced rate.

When asked how she arrived at the $55 reduced rate for the first hour, Nathan said, "There was no scientific method; it just sounded good."

To establish the $85 hourly ticket price, she had "shopped" around in her area to find out what other professionals were charging, asked herself what she felt comfortable charging, and placed herself within that range.

Dr. Robert Pritchard, professor of finance at Glassboro State College in New Jersey and one of the authors of *Strategic Marketing: A Handbook for Managers, Business Owners, and Entrepreneurs* (Addison-Wesley, 1982), likes Nathan's and

Power's first-hour approach. "I think there's a lot to be said for the adage that if a person's not willing to pay for something, they don't really want it," he says. "I'm inclined to say if they want it, they've got to expect to pay for it."

INNOVATIVE PRICING TECHNIQUES

But Pritchard sees that with competition heating up from the behemoth financial services firms for the same financial planning customers, times ahead will be tough for the smaller financial planning shop.

"I think the smaller outfit is going to have to depend very heavily on referrals," he observes. "Let's say you do financial planning for me and you charge me for the plan. Maybe we can make a deal that if I can refer a couple of people to you, the three-year checkup I would normally pay for is going to be done at a discount or for free."

"We've played with the reduced rate idea, but a few clients reacted negatively," says Rich Horowitz, principal of Weston Financial Group in Wellesley. "It didn't sit right with them."

Weston Financial, which has sixty-seven full-time employees who handle 350 ongoing clients, charges solely on a retainer basis for its financial planning services. At the end of 1986, it began to evaluate how it charged for services.

"One way is just to bill by the hour," says Horowitz, "but we rejected it. It's a system we never used. We felt we should tell a client when he comes in that this is what it's going to cost to do the job."

But pricing still was an issue with Horowitz and his partners, because, while the first year of the retainer was turning out to be very profitable, Horowitz observes, "We think maybe the second or third year is not as profitable because it's open-ended."

Horowitz and others at Weston used old statistics to figure out how much revenue each client brought in. "We found out we were doing a lot for clients that we were not charging for," says Horowitz. "So how do you price the retainer? We have to price it so we don't lose money. We're trying to find out how to make our second-year retainer profitable. We're doing research to find out what our people do."

Once Weston has established exactly how much time its professionals put into the planning process, they are going to offer clients a "full service" retainer, priced accordingly.

"We're going to say, 'If you want full service retainer, this is what it's going to cost,' " says Horowitz. "Maybe we'll offer a lesser service retainer as well, but we'll lay it all out and tell them."

MAKE PRICING STRUCTURE CLEAR

Laying it all out for the client is critical. While pricing decisions may be difficult for the planner, it's even more difficult for the prospective client if planners aren't clear about their fees.

"Maybe financial planners should be more like medical doctors and list their prices on the wall," suggests Pritchard.

Some financial advisors do just that.

Vern Woodrum, a fee-only financial planner in Charleston, South Carolina, gives each prospective client of his Resource Development Corporation a "standard fee schedule." The fee schedule is based on the client's gross income, taxes for the previous year, and gross assets. Within each of these categories, clients assign themselves a certain number of points and multiply the total by $125 to come up with the price of a financial plan.

Woodrum's point-based standard fee schedule appears on p. 189.

THE JOB-JACKET APPROACH

In *Strategic Marketing*, Pritchard and his coauthors, Bruce Bradway and Mary Anne Frenzel, write that in service industries, such as financial planning, the "job-jacket" approach to pricing—where each person working on a particular case bills out to that case—may be one of the most efficient methods of pricing, but it is not without problems.

They point out that no employee is 100 percent productive during the workday, so the unbillable time must be charged to overhead. They argue that productivity improves when each employee "keeps a record of time spent in ten- or fifteen-minute segments." They also suggest that setting standards,

Standard Fee Schedule

GROSS INCOME		TAXES		GROSS ASSETS	
INCOME	POINTS	TAXES	POINTS	ASSETS	POINTS
$25,000	4	<$5,000	0	$50,000	6
$35,000	5	$5,000	6	$100,000	7
$40,000	6	$10,000	7	$200,000	8
$50,000	7	$15,000	8	$300,000	9
$65,000	8	$20,000	9	$400,000	10
$80,000	9	$28,000	10	$500,000	11
$100,000	12	$40,000	11	$750,000	12
$125,000	13	$54,000	12	$1,000,000	13
$155,000	14	$70,000	13	$1,500,000	14
$190,000	15	$88,000	14	$2,000,000	15
$230,000	16			$2,500,000	16
$275,000	17			$3,000,000	17
$750,000	18				
$1,000,000	19				
$1,250,000	20				

Total Personal	Total Tax	Total Asset
Points = _____	Points = _____	Points = _____

GRAND TOTAL OF POINTS = _____ × $125 = _____ (TOTAL FEE)

such as "85 percent of working time must be billed to jobs," increases productivity.

Pritchard reminds us that "85 percent is a target." With a glut of lawyers in the marketplace, for instance, he suggests that "probably if most [lawyers] are at 50 percent they're doing pretty well. Many lawyers work long hours to get the number of billable hours at a reasonable level."

X TIMES THE HOURLY RATE

Pritchard, Bradway, and Frenzel also suggest that while traditionally many service businesses have billed out their time on a basis of three times the hourly rate per employee, because of inflation and rising costs of fringe benefits and computerization, the "formula during the coming decade for service businesses will be more like four times the hourly rate per employee."

Joan Powers follows the three-to-one formula for billing

out her paraplanner's time, only seven or eight hours of which are billable to clients per week. The remainder of the time she puts in during the week (around twenty-two or twenty-three hours) is billed to overhead. To meet the costs of overhead, Powers tries to have twenty billable hours a week.

Nathan shoots for a similar goal. "My goal is for twenty hours a week of billable hours, but no more," says Carol Nathan. "That's maxed out. It's actually closer to eighteen hours. When I can hit eighteen hours a week, I can hit the income stream that I want."

Unlike Powers, however, Nathan bills out her paraplanner's time at the same rate she herself charges. She contracts with clients for the number of hours she will bill them of estimated "desk time" (actually working on the plan) and puts a cap on that rate. "Meeting time is additional," Nathan explains. "Desk time is the only time I can control."

Pricing for the financial planner may vary from planner to planner based on the factors each planner uses to make pricing decisions, such as desired profit, return on investment, and cash flow; assessing the target market's reception of your price; determining the demand for your service; and evaluating competitors' prices.

When all is said and done, and a pricing structure has been established, it's up to the planner or the firm's management to decide if that structure is appropriate. Vern Woodrum, for one, thinks his price-by-point pricing system is just fine. "It's working pretty well," he says, declining specifics. "Yes sir, it's working pretty well."

20 THE FAST PITCH: *A Star Salesman Shows His Stuff*

Jim Barry talks fast. When he talks about his business, he talks even faster. He's the consummate salesman, peppering his talk with examples of how he's been able to provide solutions to people's financial problems.

"I just had a woman in today," Barry says from his Boca Raton, Florida, office, explaining he's between two clients, a tuna fish sandwich, and some yet-to-be-answered phone calls. "She's seventy-four years old, a widow, with two children. One's a college graduate who owns a little business. The other is a forty-three-year-old retarded daughter she's taken care of all of her life.... Her major problem is how does she solve the problem [of taking care of her daughter] when she crosses the great divide?"

Jim Barry works hard to sell. "I work my tail off at my business," he boasts. "I live, breathe, eat the business.... I think I have the ability to get people to believe what I'm saying to them by listening carefully to them."

One of his successful formulas is a three-pronged sales approach. Barry explains it with the precision of a man who knows his tweeters from his woofers: "I uncover the needs you've got. I disturb you. If I don't disturb you, you're going to wait forever. The third thing is, in a nice way, I tell you I think I've got a reasonable solution to the problems we uncover together."

THE ENTREPRENEURIAL INSTINCT

Barry's sales ability has built him quite a company since 1975, when he left his position as a senior vice president with Putnam Group, a mutual fund company in Boston, Massachusetts, and headed south to Boca Raton, Florida, to open the doors to the Barry Financial Group, Inc.

"Let me tell you, if I had stayed in a corporate arena, I'd still be with Putnam," explains Barry. "But I had a burning desire to be an entrepreneur. I had stepped up to the plate twice and backed down twice.... But the bottom line is the challenge, the arena, the killer instinct to get things done.... Along with that came money, obviously, but once you gain it, it's not exactly what you thought you wanted. It [money] finally gets you to the point where you can say to the world, 'Stop the merry-go-round.'"

Jim Barry followed his entrepreneurial instinct to become one of the biggest sellers of mutual funds in the business. His sales prowess has also placed his broker-dealership among the best producers in the land.

In *Financial Planning* magazine's 1986 broker-dealer survey, Asset Management Securities Corporation, Barry's broker-dealer arm, fared admirably. It was twenty-eighth on the list of broker-dealers showing the greatest growth in commissions in 1985. It was first on the list of top commissions received in 1985 by registered representatives at small financial planning broker-dealers, with its eighteen company-affiliated registered representatives earning an average of $72,288.78. And it was seventh on the list of small financial planning broker-dealers with fastest-growing limited partnership sales in 1985, with a growth of 25.55 percent.

Granted, Asset Management Securities Corporation managed to hit that number seven spot even though it only took in $23,540 in limited partnership sales that year—more than $475,000 *less* than the lowest income producer on the list, which came in at number nine in percentage growth for 1985.

The fact that Asset Management Securities Corporation only opened its doors in March 1984, and 1985 was actually its first full year of sales, was one of the significant factors that accounted for the apparently stellar growth rate.

But the fact that the growth of 1985 over 1984 is based on a year's sales vs. ten months of sales does not figure as large in Barry's sales pitch as his company's impressive growth.

GRAB SOMEONE AND SELL HIM

He loves to sell.

"You've got to be able to grab someone, get them off dead center," he says. "Marketing is not Willy Loman in *Death of a Salesman* sitting in the back room smoking cigars and telling dirty jokes. It's getting people to move."

If you were drawing up a list of those people best qualified to get people off dead center, Jim Barry would certainly be at the top. His pride in his company is evident in his talk. You may feel as if you're getting a sales pitch, but it's a pitch from a person who truly believes in the service he's offering.

"I'm not at all embarrassed by my selling skills," says Barry. "Remember, you're selling every day. You've got to motivate. You've got to be selling. Life is built on selling a concept. Don't be afraid to sell."

SELLING THE CONCEPT

When your selling skills draw in a total of 3,000 clients, as Barry's have done, that's certainly nothing to be embarrassed by.

Jim Barry is sold on the concept of financial planning, and in turn he sells his clients on it. But rather than convince them he knows all the answers, Barry convinces them he knows where to find the answers.

His pitch combines complimenting potential clients on their professional prowess with telling them they should rely on others with equal professional prowess to manage their money. The pitch goes something like this: "When a person comes in to me and owns thirty stocks and some bonds, they are in effect their own mutual fund. How can you be a money manager and a doctor at the same time? Most of us should not be physically managing our money on a daily basis. Our job is to be the guider of you to find the right money manager to do the job right.

"I had a client . . . who's an open heart surgeon from Ft. Lauderdale, I told him, 'There's no way you'd ever operate on me. You know it would be my luck that the day you were going to operate on me the Dow Jones Industrial Average would be down 40 points. Would your mind be on the market or on my heart?' "

DELEGATE
RESPONSIBILITY
AND SELL

But how does Barry, who estimates that only 10 to 15 percent of his 3,000-person client base are product-only–type clients, manage to do financial planning for 2,500-plus? How much contact can he have with his clients?

"People see me all the time," says Barry. "If you're going

to build an organization, you've got to delegate responsibility. When you become a client, you are assigned a person on our staff. I normally end up involved with maybe seven or eight clients a day. We have eighteen people who are Series 7 registered, probably fourteen of them are going through the CFP program. We have very strong administrative assistants."

Barry believes that delegating responsibility not only helps him handle the massive client load but also builds the expertise of his staff. "I wake up every morning realizing what I don't know about my business," he says. "If we're going to build a national company, then that company's going to be geared to selling on the line. I am not going to do that by being one-on-one all the time [with clients]. I'm also building a staff that can deal with clients."

"I'm extremely disciplined in my office," Barry explains, when asked how he sells so much. "I have my appointments starting at 9 running through sometimes to 6 at night. I'm programmed. . . . I give my clients my home number. I'm reachable. And you know, I get very few calls at home."

Barry explains his commitment to clients by explaining how he is there for clients. On the Friday of a long weekend, one of Barry's doctor clients had returned from a visit to Germany. Barry and his group had done a fact-finding for the doctor before his visit.

"Well here it is Friday, when a lot of my friends in Boston took the long holiday," says Barry. "We're in here Friday at 4 in the afternoon, and he's writing out a check for $650,000 when other people are riding out to the Cape. So that's commitment, isn't it?" Barry asks, quickly adding with a laugh, "or I'm a nut."

"We're very much client oriented," Barry insists. "If I've got one major strength, it's the ability to market our services. I'm able to get the person excited. Take charge of your life type of thing. I do that through radio and television and through seminars. I average about two speaking engagements a month. Plus that's fun. That keeps me in touch with the realities of life."

EDUCATING CLIENTS

Barry argues that his "bottom line is first of all teaching people how to make a living. It's one thing to make money, a whole other to manage money. They [clients] don't understand even the language we use as financial planners. It's an education process."

To educate clients, Barry Financial Group organizes monthly seminars. "We educate our clients on an ongoing basis," explains Barry. "We have an all-day workshop, for which we bring in people from various financial arenas. [They are held] once a month starting at 8:30 in the morning and run to 4:30 in the afternoon. We average between 300 and 400 clients. We let our clients invite one other person. If they're a client of mine and I've done a good job of leading them along, I understand marketing enough to know I've got some stature there."

Barry doesn't want to make his clients geniuses. He also doesn't think they should be overloaded with information. Ask him how much he thinks is enough about mutual funds to cover the topic at one of his seminars and he'll say: "What enough is in a mutual fund session is: 'What is a mutual fund to begin with? How is it set up? What is the purpose behind it? How does it work? What's the purpose of diversification?' "

BELIEVE IN THE PRODUCT

"I believe in mutual funds," says Barry. "I don't think there's too much money pouring into mutual funds. We've finally become aware that we can have our money managed down to $2,000."

Barry does believe, however, that some of the larger mutual funds, particularly those that have grown to billions of dollars in assets, present potential problems. "I believe the bigger the fund, the more problems the money manager is going to have," says Barry. "I think they should look at what one fund manager in an individual fund can reasonably manage. The bigger the fund, the more headaches in liquidity on the downside."

Jim Barry's belief in mutual funds stems from his days with Putnam, where he first decided to go into financial planning.

"The reason I got into financial planning," recalls Barry, "is that as I was traveling when I was with Putnam, it [the situation in the financial services field] was like the guy in [the movie] *Network*. [The newscaster in *Network* tells people to stick their heads out their windows and yell, 'I'm mad as hell, and I'm not going to take it anymore.'] People were fed up. The guy's scratching his head saying, 'What the hell is this guy saying to me?'

"The best things don't come from the ivory towers of the world or Putnam or the Barry Group. They come from the public recognizing a need.

"I can remember seventeen years ago running seminars on financial planning. I said [to others in the financial services industry] 'You're going to be Willy Loman if you don't understand total account selling.' The public was saying there must be a better method. . . . There was a need there. At the same time, there was also a need in the mind of the younger person coming up in the business. Is there a better method? At the same time, the association [International Association for Financial Planning] was being put together. It was a cross-pollination of different ideas."

SERVICE THE NEEDS OF
THE CLIENT

Barry is the first to admit that not everyone is a potential client for financial planning. Take the 10 to 15 percent of his client base that only buy product, for instance. He says, "I can think of a client who is a janitor in a high school. He's got a total of $25,000. What he needs is just a little miniplan."

To fulfill the financial planning function when clients do need it, the Barry Financial Group is set up to give advice, sell insurance, sell securities through its broker-dealer arm, and do most every other aspect of financial planning except for taxes and trusts.

"The only place we network is with CPAs and trust officers," says Barry. "We don't do trusts or will planning or incorporate the fellow. We direct them to good attorneys out there who can do the job for them."

LEARNING FROM
MISTAKES

In spite of his success record and his ability to talk ad infinitum on all aspects of the Barry Financial Group's mission, Barry admits that some of his savvy comes from having learned from the mistakes he made early on running his business.

"Hell, I made all kinds of mistakes. Probably the third year in business I had a payroll of over 400,000 bucks, and that's not counting me. I found myself having a lot of people, and I thought I needed no incentives. But the only one marketing was me.

"Now, when every dollar bill comes into this company I take a percentage. We say, here's what we've historically been doing, every bit, whether it be the planning end or the broker-dealer end. I come up with a percentage of that. Then I have key people [to whom] I assign [bonuses on] a point system. . . . I give points to different people who know in advance what they're going to get based on the profits of the company. I want the ability to say, 'Here's a bonus.' So there are incentives involved. Our receptionists answer very nicely here because we've got incentives."

Jim Barry doesn't mind at all giving away part of his profits in the form of incentive bonuses. "I'd rather own a small piece of a monster pie than a large piece of a small pie," he explains.

The monster pie promises to get larger as Asset Management Securities Corporation's commissions from sales continue to supplement the fees from Barry's financial planning service.

SHARING IDEAS

Barry also believes in sharing his ideas with others in the business. "Don't be afraid of sharing ideas with your peers in the business, because there's so much business," he explains.

Besides, people may get similar advice elsewhere, Barry humbly reckons, but they won't get Jim Barry.

Barry's boast that his "skill is as a communicator" convinces. He uses that skill to sell at every turn. "I've spent time over the past twenty-five years learning what selling is about," he says. "I still have to sell my wife on what it is we're doing here, for God's sake."

21 THE PSYCHOLOGY OF SELLING:
"Subliminal" Selling Skills

Not everyone is a Jim Barry. Not everybody has his gift of gab, the special skill needed to effectively pitch a client. For those who are not blessed with such traits, Dr. Kerry Johnson offers an option: subliminal selling skills.

In August, many of the more upscale psychologists in Manhattan go on vacation, leaving thousands of therapy clients to fend for themselves in a city of countless phobias. During August, while some of the more fashionable shrinks may summer in the Hamptons, Dr. Kerry Johnson will present seminars to eleven different groups in California, Montana, Washington, Wisconsin, Kansas, and whereabouts yet to be determined.

But Kerry Johnson is not an ordinary psychologist. Based in Santa Ana, California, he caters to financial services organizations that are in the selling business. Using the concept of "neurolinguistic programming" as the basis for his training sessions, Johnson teaches his seminar attendees how to communicate with their clients by talking to them in their primary mode of expression.

Babe Ruth may have been the Sultan of Swat; Kerry Johnson, who "did 150 dates" last year, is the Psychologist of Sell.

NONMANIPULATIVE CONTROL

One of the basic premises of neurolinguistic programming, developed by Richard Bandler and John Grinder and spelled out in their book, *Frogs Into Princes* (Real People Press, 1979), is that people have one primary mode of expression—visual, auditory, or kinesthetic. By identifying the mode a person operates in and matching that mode by using appropriate verbs and expressions, you can gain rapport with that person and increase the chances of effective communication.

Johnson calls this "subliminal selling," which might suggest some underhanded manipulative technique, but, says Johnson, "It's as ethical as selling a mutual fund that could sometimes collapse. The ethics start with you."

Bandler and Grinder call themselves *modelers*, as opposed to manipulators. "The function of modeling," they write, "is to arrive at descriptions which are *useful*. . . . We're not offering you something that's *true*, just things that are *useful*."

203

"I don't see it as manipulating at all," says Johnson. "Financial planners are such atrocious communicators that we're just bringing them up to acceptable levels."

When Johnson talks about communication, he talks about it "from the standpoint that we're really trying to figure out what the client really needs and what they really want and giving it to him."

SUBLIMINAL SELLING BASICS

The basics of Johnson's subliminal selling technique are simple. First, identify the client's primary mode of expression. You can do this first by watching your client's eyes.

Visuals will tend to look up to the left when recollecting or reconstructing events and up to the right when thinking in the future or constructing events. They will tend to look straight ahead, unfocused, when they are contemplating ideas, making mental pictures in their heads.

Auditories will look to the left side when reconstructing and to the right side when constructing.

Kinesthetics will tend to look down to the right when thinking about the response to a question.

IDENTIFYING THE MODE OF EXPRESSION

By asking a question as simple as "How many times do you hear the word 'lamb' in the nursery rhyme 'Mary Had a Little Lamb,'" you can watch a person's eyes and identify his or her primary mode of expression.

There is some variance if a person is left-handed, but Johnson says that only 10 to 11 percent of left-handed people reverse the eye movements.

"You can usually calibrate the client depending on whether they're left- or right-handed," he says. "I'll ask you about that book you wrote, or maybe something that happened with a magazine [article you wrote]. If I see you consistently look up to the right, which is constructive creating, when you should be recalling, you could be switching. Up to the left is

recalling past images or past hearing. Up to the right is visual-
izing or creating, constructing future images. Over to the right
side . . . is creating auditory sounds in the future. So what's
happening there is if I see you consistently look up to the right
when you should be going up left, for example, with things
about your background, either . . . you're lying, or . . . you're
telling the truth and [are] left-handed with that 10 percent of
the left-handers who will do that."

MATCH PREDICATES AND
THE FEEL, FELT, FOUND
TECHNIQUE

Once you've identified your client's primary expressive mode,
you want to "match predicates."

With visuals, Johnson suggests you use words like *show,
picture, looks, see, view, bright, clear,* and *perspective.* With
auditories, use words like *tone, static, hear, sounds,* and *say.*
With kinesthetics, use words like *touch base, rub, feel,* and
handle.

Johnson points out that the subliminal selling techniques
he teaches, while based on neurolinguistic programming, are
not all that new or all that difficult. "There's an old sales
training technique that a lot of these financial planners learn
when they're stockbrokers or insurance agents called the 'feel,
felt, found technique,' " he says.

When a client complains about the expense of a particular
service or product, Johnson explains, the professional says,
"Well, I understand how you *feel.* . . . I had a client who *felt*
that same way last week until he *found* that . . . ."

Feel, felt, found works for the kinesthetic, while *see, saw,
found* works for the visual, and *hear, said, found* for auditories.

RECOGNIZING THE NEED
FOR ADVANCED SALES
SUPPORT

Johnson is on the road a lot. His 150 dates a year keep him on
the road 200 days a year. But it's a lifestyle he grew accustomed
to when he played on the professional tennis circuit from 1976
to 1978.

"I wasn't great," he says, adding, "I was up to ninety-fifth in the world. I think there's about 1,500 [players] in the ATP [Association of Tennis Professionals]. I was there [ninety-fifth place] for two weeks."

Johnson completed his PhD in psychology and then began working as a consulting psychologist to various companies.

"You know how I started doing this kind of stuff?" Johnson says when asked about how he got into the seminar business. "It was kind of funny, because during the time I was consulting I found out that [companies] were just throwing their new prospective agents against the wall and saying 'Hey, if you really make it, you'll do well, and you really won't if you can't.' They were leaving the two- to twenty-year people out there on their own. There was just no training for them. They weren't getting the benefits of support. . . .

"So I said to these guys, 'You know you ought to start doing some advanced sales support for these people, cause that's where your business in later life is going to come from,' which is true. They're selling securities now. They're brokering products. I started speaking to NALU functions—National Association of Life Underwriters—to association leaders and also to general agency managers' groups to try to get consulting business from other companies.

"I started speaking, and nobody ever asked me to consult for some reason. But they asked me to come back and speak to their agencies and regional association meetings."

Johnson, who gets $2,500 for one of his programs plus whatever he makes on the six audio- and videotapes he sells to seminar attendees, now lists among the financial services clients he's worked with Anchor National, First Affiliated, Private Ledger, Centennial, Equitec, August Financial, and Kagin's Numismatics.

Because Johnson will sometimes waive his fee to an association if he is doing a presentation, a financial services wholesaler or retailer will occasionally underwrite the fee. At a recent presentation at the New England Regional Conference for Financial Planning, Kagin's underwrote the program. "Actually I'm doing a trade-out," says Johnson. "I'm taking my fee in rare coins."

During his presentation Johnson will tell the audience that Kagin's is sponsoring his program. Whenever it's appropriate and he needs to use a product example in his presentation, he'll use the example of Kagin's. Johnson doesn't sell for Kagin's or any other organization. They underwrite his presentation and receive a little publicity in return.

"The real estate companies, the mutual fund companies, and everybody else are becoming incredibly competitive," says Johnson. "Through the IAFP symposiums that I've been doing and most of the chapter meetings, there are always . . . double the number of usual attendees that will come to hear my program. . . . It's because they want these kind of skills. They want that kind of programming.

"So what I've done is I've gone to the wholesalers and I've said to them, 'You know a lot of these IAFP chapters and some of these seminar groups don't have a lot of money. That's your marketplace. What do you think if you sponsor me, pay my fees, so we can go to that marketplace?

"It's funny, but almost every program I do now is sponsored by a wholesaler, almost every single one."

THE SIZZLE

Johnson's presentations typically include an hour on one of many different aspects of sales psychology, which include subliminal selling, how to read your client's mind, and the psychology of productivity. There is real substance to his presentations, but he is also a consummate entertainer. The presentations are peppered with one-liners, audience heckling, and snappy interchange with audience members.

"You know I never lost track that Johnny Carson once said that people will pay much more to be entertained than they will ever pay to be educated," says Johnson. "If you ever lose track, then you'd be lumped in with those academics. So I've got to keep a lot of sizzle in it."

Johnson estimates that when he first started doing his presentations, about 60 percent was sizzle, 40 percent was steak. "Now, I think as I mature," he says, "I care less about the snazziness and the sizzle, and I'd say now about 70 to 80 percent is steak and 20 percent is sizzle.

"The sales psychologist stuff is sizzle, you know it is. . . . My marketplace realizes that you need to be that way to make it. They do the same thing."

Even though Johnson, at the beginning of his presentation,

glibly promises to give you "ideas to put more bread on your table and BMWs in your driveway," for professionals who are looking for a manipulation tool that will make clients beg them to sell them more, more, more, what Johnson presents in his sales psychology seminars will probably not be their cup of tea.

If, however, professionals are looking for effective ways to improve communication skills, they might be able to take what Dr. Johnson says about identifying primary expressive modes and apply it.

GIVE THE CLIENTS WHAT THEY WANT

While the principles Johnson sets out in his subliminal selling seminars eschew obfuscation, they are not without rules. One of the more common mistakes that Johnson's IAFP seminar audiences in both Anaheim and Boston made was to try to match a person's primary expressive mode before finding out what it was.

For example, when Johnson had people pair off and try to sell one another a fountain pen, many of the audience participants neglected to ask their prospective buyer what they considered to be the ideal pen. Such a question would result in the seller's being able to determine from the buyer's eye movement that person's primary expressive mode.

Crucial to the success of Johnson's subliminal selling process is that you give the client what he or she wants. "When you close too hard, when you manipulate, you'll sell that day, but they'll give it back to you," says Johnson.

"Make sure that they want what they want. Make sure that you give them something that they're happy with, that they can live with when they go to sleep that night, [that] when they've forgotten all about your techniques they really feel good about the relationship with you, and more important, that the trust is there, and they're getting the best possible solution."

22 GRABBING HOLD OF THE BIG PICTURE: *Use Muppet Meeting Films and Your Meetings Will Never Be the Same*

A serious message can come in what seems to be a silly package, but people will listen to it. Anyone who has tried to sell anything at a seminar knows the value of humor.

How many times has something like this happened to you at a training seminar or sales convention? You walk into the room, find your seat, and wait for the speaker. The screen and projector, flipchart, and other accoutrements are all in place. The speaker takes the podium.

He starts by saying something like, "Here in our company we try to simplify things for you." Right away you know you're in trouble. You came to learn how to market your services or develop your product and you just know that this guy, in his effort to simplify, is going to make your business life miserable.

Sure enough, he starts in with acronym after acronym designed to make your life easier, smoother. It all adds up to Package Line Analysis Nexus or Business Improvement Guarantee—the BIG PLAN. Sound all too familiar?

Well, maybe not. But if you happen upon a session run by one of the thousands of companies that use Muppet Meeting Films for a refreshing change of pace in their meetings, you won't be surprised to hear Leo, the corporate Muppet, up at the podium expounding on just such a BIG PLAN in one of four segments of *The Muppet Breakthrough Film.*

THE BREAK AT TRAINING SESSIONS

Leo and Grump are two of the Muppets developed especially for the Muppet Meeting Films, a series of films designed for the corporate market by Henson Associates in New York City. The films are packaged with three or four two- to four-minute segments on each reel or tape. Typically, there will be segments that meeting planners can use for introducing a speaker, taking a break, or wrapping up a meeting or session.

Currently there are seven Muppet Meeting Films. They're all available in 16-millimeter or videocassette format. The cost for previewing the films is $25. To rent one costs $250; to buy, $495.

Nearly every Fortune 500 company owns at least one of the films. Many financial services institutions find they are wonderful tools to use when holding training sessions for their sales and marketing forces.

"We use them at a couple of sales conventions a year," says David Vanselow, assistant vice president of sales promotion for the Franklin Life Insurance Company, based in Springfield, Illinois, which had in excess of $6 billion in sales of life insurance and annuity products and assets of more than $3.5 billion in 1985.

Vanselow plans Franklin Life's sales meetings. "We've also used the Muppet films at a couple of smaller regional meetings and training sessions where our sales associates come in for a technical training program," he says. "Complicated concepts are thrown at the associates at these sessions, so we use the Muppets to lessen the tension and perhaps some of the drudgery."

With financial advisors and other financial services professionals being called upon more and more to run or attend many professional seminars or day-long training sessions, savvy film producers are supplying that market with what might best be called "corporate training relief films" Jim Henson's Muppet films are just one example. British comedian, actor, and former Monty Python television show star John Cleese also recently released a series of films targeted at the corporate market.

In both cases, the films are light. They're not meant to teach you or your clients about internal rate of return or the effective use of hedging in the stock options market. Rather, they're designed specifically to "lighten up" meetings where such discussions take place.

FROM BIG BLUE
TO BIG MUPPETS

The Muppet Meeting Films were born more than ten years ago when David Lazer, an executive with IBM, approached Jim Henson, the famed Muppet creator, about developing a series of films to liven up IBM meetings. The custom-made films for IBM were successful, and Lazer joined Henson Associates as a vice president and executive producer. Word of mouth began to spread the news through corporate America. The result was the development of generic films that could be used by all companies.

Early on, many of the same Muppet characters who graced the screen in the Muppet movies and The Muppet Show on television were also characters in the Muppet Meeting Films. Kermit the Frog serves as corporate spokesfrog. In fact, when they were introducing a new film by advertising in *The Wall Street Journal* last January, it was Kermit's likeness that graced the ad space, replete with director's chair and megaphone.

There's also a "Rod-Serling-type" character who was introduced in the "Safety Zone" segment of the *Muppet Lift-Off Film*. The piece is a takeoff on the old "Twilight Zone" television series, and the model for the physical likeness of this Muppet character was reportedly David Lazer.

But the true stars of the Muppet Meeting Films are the two characters designed specifically for the film series, Leo and Grump. Together, the two of them represent most every gung-ho corporate man and every grumpy doubting cohort you'll ever remember or meet.

About the only complaint that most Muppet Meeting Film users seem to have is that they don't turn them out fast enough. Leigh Cloniger, manager of the Muppet Meeting Films division of Henson Associates, understands the problem. "A lot of people use them on the same audiences year after year, so there's a demand for new films" she says. "Plus, I just like getting a new product out there."

But, Cloniger adds, "Because Jim's committed to so many different projects, we have to work around his schedule. Last time we did six different segments in two days."

What many people may forget is that the Muppets are "brought to life" by specific actors who control the voices and actions of specific Muppet creations. Jim Henson (who is also the voice of Kermit) is Leo in the Muppet Meeting Films; Frank Oz (of Miss Piggy fame) is Grump.

REACHING THE
CORPORATE MARKET

"But while Jim is committed to feature films and television specials," says Cloniger, "he also likes these films, because they reach a segment of the population that nothing else we do reaches. One thing Jim's done is to let people know his name stands for quality. People know that. And they'll look at [the Muppet Meeting Films] based on that alone. He would like to do something that would appeal to anybody. 'The Muppet

Show' wasn't just for children. In his films and television he doesn't ever want to limit the audience. A lot of people might think that because they're puppets, they're for kids. In the business world, we can get to them and show them that this just isn't so."

If the experience of Sarah Gurtis is any indication, Cloniger has "gotten to them." Gurtis is vice president of marketing for Sun Bank, Inc. (headquartered in Orlando, Florida) which has $1 billion in assets and more than 300 offices around the state. She says, "We've used the films in our ongoing training sessions. We've used them in the new accounts area, at senior executive retreats, at seminars with outside people. They're such a nice diversion—and so well done. A couple of banks have used them in Chamber [of Commerce] presentations, mostly to lead into coffee breaks. They're an incredibly good way to pace a meeting."

Cloniger runs the entire Muppet Meeting Film division of Henson Associates with her assistant, Sandy Cattani, fielding requests from sometimes 200 different companies a month. Her office in a brownstone on East 69th Street in Manhattan features a framed Art of Muppets poster on a wall behind her desk and Muppet Babies Feeding Sets stashed behind the couch. She points out, "The films are typically not good for a one-hour meeting. Three hours or longer, and certainly day-long meetings, would be more appropriate."

USERS INFLUENCE NEW MUPPET FILM RELEASES

Every three years, Cloniger will do a survey of her film users to get an idea of what kinds of topics they would like covered. "The films have to fill some function or people would not feel comfortable using them," she says. "They're not only a light touch but can be used as a kind of tool when the meeting is going on."

Cloniger also realizes the pressure on meeting planners to run successful meetings. "The end result," she says, "is that if he [the meeting planner] can make the audience laugh and delight them, it's only going to reflect on him. People tend to be uptight at meetings, and these films tend to relax."

In her surveys, Cloniger has found that most of the films

are used for training in sales, promotion, and marketing. "The customer list is very loyal," she says, holding up a 5-inch-thick binder of users' names on a computer printout. "They'll often buy multiple copies."

The bulk of the customer list consists of companies with more than 500 employees, featuring such corporations as Consolidated Capital Companies, Integrated Capital Services, Citicorp, Chemical Bank, Paine Webber, Merrill Lynch, Smith Barney, Dean Witter, Kidder Peabody, Chase Manhattan, IDS, and The New England. But Cloniger says that more and more smaller groups are buying the films. In fact, quite a few church groups have purchased the films lately.

While the films are available in both videocassette and 16-millimeter-film format, 90 percent of the film users choose 16-millimeter. Cloniger attributes this to technology. "I think the films are more effective on a big screen," she says. "Three years ago, the videocassette users could use small monitors around the room at a meeting. Technology now looks good for developing a big screen [for videocassette projection], but the majority of our films are still 16-millimeter. We're going to have to change our ways in two to three years when technology catches up."

In the meantime, the Muppet Meeting Films seem to be meeting with a very positive, if sometimes unusual, response. A story is told about Apple Computer executives imitating a scene from the "Grump Critic" segment of the *Gimme a Break* Muppet film. In the segment, Leo asks Grump to honk every time his speech gets boring. The upshot of the segment is that there's a lot of honking going on. It seems that Apple executives came armed with horns to one of their own sessions. Reports were that no one was bored at the meeting.

The Muppet Perk-Up Film is one of the newest of the Muppet Meeting Films. Cloniger played the video in her office. A wooden block on the tape machine that Cloniger put the videocassette into says, "I want to help you out. Which way did you come in?"

The new film features three segments: "The Half-Minute Manager," a spoof of the *One-Minute Manager* (or "microwave management," as Larry Grimes, a professor at Bethany College in West Virginia, calls it); "Benefits," which pokes fun at company benefit policies; and "Nobody's Perfect," on the search for the perfect employee.

Leo and Grump are again the stars in the new film segments. Leo is the gung-ho enthusiast. It's Leo who stands at the podium in an early Muppet Meeting Film titled *The Final Speech* and starts bestowing wondrous praise on his audience, the veterans and the bright young people—"You are our future." The music swells; the enthusiasm builds. Finally it comes down to one word, Leo tells us. And that word is *Sell*. The music is at full crescendo. Leo loses control telling his audience to "sell their socks off." It's no wonder the film has become known as "Sell, Sell, Sell," rather than by its original title.

The Muppet Meeting Films will not answer your due diligence questions, nor will they streamline your practice into a lean, mean profit-making machine. If used in appropriate settings, however, they just might give you, your colleagues, and your clients the opportunity to relax, breathe easy for a moment, and gain perspective on the bigger picture. In this respect, they're a great marketing tool, because the end result could be that you'll enjoy what you're doing a bit more and pass that enjoyment on to your clients.

On Cloniger's office wall is a framed picture of Grump. She points to the picture and says, "There's Grump right there. Isn't he a darling?" Obviously a woman who loves her work.

23 BUILD ME A PRACTICE: *Using Seminars to Build a Financial Advisory Firm*

Vern Hayden's father was a minister who, when Vern was growing up, used to move every four or five years.

"His thing was to build churches," says Hayden, who cofounded Independent Financial Services, Inc., in White Plains, New York, in 1983 and now has a personal financial planning practice with DESCAP and a consulting firm called Financial Services Advisory Company in Westport, Connecticut.

When Hayden and cofounders decided to start IFS in 1983, Hayden, who is a CFP and a member of the International Association for Financial Planning's Registry of Financial Planning Practitioners, had a flourishing financial planning practice that he had begun in San Rafael, California, seventeen years earlier. But like his father, Hayden likes to build things. In the younger Hayden's case, it's financial planning practices rather than churches. Even when he was working with his 150 or so clients in San Rafael, Hayden ran a series of training programs for people entering the financial planning field.

"I ran seminars in Nevada, California, and Utah, among other places," recalls Hayden. "The training program would give them the direction they needed. My purpose was not only to work with them but to attract a client base and leave them with clients."

BUILDING CREDIBILITY

So when Hayden and his partners were developing the business plan for IFS, which was to be based in White Plains, because, Hayden says, "Westchester County was a great market, virtually untapped for financial planning," they decided that seminars would be integral to getting the client base they needed to build their practice.

"We had the ambition of trying to build credibility in a short period of time," says Hayden. "The purpose of the seminar is to establish a good client base plus lead to referrals. It's also a way of refurbishing the client base."

When he moved East, Hayden sold his San Rafael practice, which a former "junior partner" now runs, to IFS. The president of IFS, Andrew Swart, also merged his Dallas practice into IFS when he moved up to White Plains in 1985.

Free educational seminars were to be the lure that would

draw in clients for the newly established IFS. The approach worked, and by mid-1986 IFS boasted a staff of thirty professionals and administrative personnel. Hayden recalls that there were about eight other financial consultants in addition to himself and that "company-wide there [were] probably 1,300 to 1,400 clients of all kinds." IFS planners work on a fee-plus-commission basis.

Hayden ran most of the seminars, bringing in other speakers only occasionally. In 1984, he ran sixty-eight seminars, which had an average attendance of ninety-seven people, or sixty-seven "client units," a tag Hayden uses to categorize husband-and-wife attendees.

The number of seminars dropped to twelve in 1985. Because IFS had successfully established an initial base of clients, it wasn't necessary to run as many seminars as they had in 1984, their first full year of operation.

"The time to get out of the seminar business is when you've established a mature practice," says Hayden. He figures that a hundred upscale clients is enough for the individual planner, a market he defines as consisting of businesspeople, professionals such as doctors and lawyers, and corporate executives.

Using seminars, IFS had been able to build a solid client base for the White Plains office, a 10,000-square-foot building that serves as headquarters for the practice.

EXPERIMENTATION
FOR EFFECTIVENESS

Many financial advisors find that seminars are a good way to gain exposure in their communities and attract new clients. Few do it with quite the expertise and, more importantly, the profitability that Hayden brought to IFS.

His seminars were held on only one night because Hayden experimented and found that there was little difference in the effectiveness of one-night or four-night-long seminars. "In fact, we had some fallout among attendees with multiple nights," says Hayden.

This experimentation for effectiveness is typical of most aspects of the seminars Hayden runs. His costs are broken down to the minutest details, even the cookies served. He admits, however, that "refreshments are not necessary. It's just a nice extra to have. I dare say it doesn't affect the return."

THE COSTS

It costs between $4,000 and $4,500 for Hayden to run one of his seminars. And some may wonder how they can be profitable if he offers them for free. The answer, of course, is in the ultimate revenues received from clients attracted. Hayden's track record with clients is impressive. On the average, 67 percent of the attendees request interviews. Of those, almost 50 percent become clients. With costs running $4,000 to $4,500, revenues from clients attracted by a given seminar ultimately ran to around $43,000, a profit margin of more than $38,000.

Hayden points out that "the profits on seminars will show over a twelve-month period. It takes almost a full year to know the results of a seminar in terms of revenue."

CHECKLISTS AND STRATEGIES

Hayden uses detailed checklists for his seminars to make sure they'll come off without a hitch. He calls the main one a "Task Flow Checklist for Financial Planning Seminar," and it details everything that has to be done in the eight weeks leading to the seminar. From selecting a date and ordering mailing lists in the first week to verifying who the proper contact person at the facility will be in the final week, it's all covered. He uses facility checklists to make sure everything's been prepared according to specification at the facility. And he's got his handouts printed and ready to pass out by the night of the show.

Very little is overlooked. Hayden even has his own portable speaker system, just in case the facility can't provide him with one. At the sessions he runs for other planners interested in putting on seminars, Hayden recommends Lectrosonics, Inc., in Albuquerque, New Mexico, for their wireless lavaliere mike system called the Freedom Mike.

Hayden's very free about sharing his success strategies with competing financial planners. In addition to his work as a financial planner, now at DESCAP, he also does consulting work through his Financial Services Advisory Company. "If somebody wanted to open across the street, I'd probably help them out," says Hayden. He says his fees are generally $2,000 a day plus expenses.

Hayden is doing a lot right when it comes to running a seminar. The response rate to the direct mail invitations he sends out comes to more than 2 percent, which is quite respectable for a direct mail campaign trying to attract upscale clients.

PROFIT AND LOSS

But perhaps the most impressive thing about the way Hayden runs his seminars is his precision in calculating profit and loss. While many planners would agree that running seminars was a good thing to build a client base, few would probably know exactly how good or profitable a thing it really was.

"The feeling I've got is that there aren't too many planners who are also great administrators," notes Hayden. "It's the old story about the entrepreneur knowing how to get a business going but needing to bring in professional management."

The breakdown of costs, revenues, and profits for a "composite" Hayden seminar runs something like this:

Costs

ITEM	PER UNIT	TOTAL
Facility	—	$200
Insurance	—	—
Invitations	.06	$360
Reply Cards	.065	$390
Envelopes	.08	$480
Addressing & Stuffing	.175	$1,050
Receptionists (2)	$25	$50
Refreshments	$1	$120
Signs	$2.50	$7.50
Handouts	$1.20	$144
Postage	.22	$1,320
Police/Student Parking Guide	$20	$60
Confirmation Letter & Env.	.14	$16.80
Postage	.22	$26.40
TOTAL	$50.66	$4,224.70

Revenues

ITEM	NUMBER	PERCENT
Number of Mailings	6,000	—
Replies	129	2.3
Attendees	97	75
Client Units (Husbands & Wives Count as 1 Unit)	67	
Requesting Interviews	44	67
Actual Interviews	33	72
Clients	21	65

SOURCE	AMOUNT	TOTAL
Counseling Fees	$700	$14,700
Commissions		
Securities	1,050	22,050
Insurance	300	6,300
Total Revenue Per Seminar		$43,050

Profits

Total Revenue	$43,050.00
Total Costs	$4,224.70
Profits	$38,825.30

By carefully structuring seminars, experimenting with what works and what doesn't work, and monitoring costs and revenues, Hayden and his partners and staff at IFS were able to run seminars that effectively built a solid client base for IFS in less than two years.

The success pleases Hayden. "My dad was a builder," he says. "I kind of feel like I'm a builder too."

RESOURCES

American Association of Personal Financial Planners (AAPFP), 21031 Ventura Boulevard, Suite 903, Woodland Hills, California 91364, 818-348-5400.

American Institute of Certified Public Accountants (AICPA), 1211 Avenue of the Americas, New York, New York 10036-8775, 212-575-6200.

Atrium Publishing, 1615 Northern Boulevard, Manhasset, New York 11030, 516-365-7144.

College for Financial Planning, 9725 East Hampden Avenue, Denver, Colorado 80231, 303-755-7101.

Direct Response: The Digest of Direct Marketing, Box 2100, Rolling Hills Estates, California 90274, 213-373-9408.

The Editor and Publisher Market Guide, published annually by Editor and Publisher Co., Inc., 575 Lexington Ave., New York, New York, 10022, 212-752-7050.

Financial Planning: The Magazine for Financial Services Professionals, published monthly by the Financial Services Information Company, a subsidiary of the International Association for Financial Planning, $5 per issue; annual subscription, $48. Two Concourse Parkway, Suite 800, Atlanta, Georgia 30328, 404-395-1605.

The Freedom Mike. Lectrosonics, Inc., Box 12617, Albuquerque, New Mexico 87915-0617, 800-821-1121.

Institute of Certified Financial Planners (ICFP), 3443 South Galena, Suite 190, Denver, Colorado 80231, 303-751-7600.

International Association for Financial Planning (IAFP), Two Concourse Parkway, Suite 800, Atlanta, Georgia 30328, 404-395-1605.

Leonard Financial Software, Box 13990, Research Triangle Park, North Carolina 27709, 800-632-3044.

Liberty Publishing, Inc., 199 Newbury St., Suite 118, Danvers, Massachusetts 01923, 617-777-5000, 800-722-7270.

Longman Financial Services Publishing, 520 North Dearborn Street, Chicago, Illinois 60610, 800-428-3846 (800-654-8596 in Illinois).

Market Master. Binary Systems, 173 California Street, Newton, Massachusetts 02158, 617-527-7944.

Muppet™ Meeting Films. Henson Associates, Inc., Department s 887, 117 East 69th Street, New York, New York 10021, 212-861-1360.

NameBase, 620 Belmont Avenue, Indianapolis, Indiana 46221, 317-639-2289.

New England Financial Advisors, 501 Boylston Street, Boston, Massachusetts 02117, 800-343-7506.

O'Dwyer's Directory of Public Relations Executives, published annually by J. R. O'Dwyer Co., Inc., 271 Madison Ave., New York, New York 10016, 212-679-2471

Pro-Mail, 415 Silas Deane Highway, Wethersfield, Connecticut 06109, 203-721-8929.

ProPlan, Confidential Planning Services, 2507 North Verity Parkway, Middleton, Ohio 45042, 513-424-1656.

Reston Financial Publishing, Inc., 1850 Centennial Park Drive, Suite 300, Reston, Virginia 22091, 703-860-8400.

Registry of Financial Planning Practitioners. International Association for Financial Planning, Two Concourse Parkway, Suite 800, Atlanta, Georgia 30328, 404-395-1605.

The Selkirk Correspondent. The Market Planning Group, 80 Boylston Street, Suite 1207, Boston, Massachusetts 02116, 617-542-4417.

Softbridge Microsystems Corporation, 125 Cambridge Park Drive, Cambridge, Massachusetts 02140, 800-325-6060 (800-325-5959 in Massachusetts).

Sterling Wentworth Corporation, 2319 Foothill Drive, Suite 150, Salt Lake City, Utah 84109, 800-752-6637.

BIBLIOGRAPHY

"The American Dream." Survey conducted by the Roper Organization for *The Wall Street Journal*, February 1987.

"Americans Cope with Their Finances." Survey conducted by the International Association for Financial Planning, 1987.

BANDLER, RICHARD, AND JOHN GRINDER. *Frogs Into Princes: Neuro-Linguistic Programming.* Moab, UT: Real People Press, 1979.

BERG, BARBARA J. *The Crisis of the Working Mother.* New York: Summit Books, 1986.

BRADWAY, BRUCE M., ROBERT E. PRITCHARD, AND MARY ANNE FRENZEL. *Strategic Marketing: A Handbook for Managers, Business Owners, and Entrepreneurs.* Reading, MA: Addison-Wesley, 1982.

BRILES, JUDITH. *Money Phases: The Six Financial Stages of a Woman's Life.* New York: Simon and Schuster, 1984.

COLLETTI, DEBORAH L., MARJOLIJN VAN DER VELDER, AND JEFFREY L. SEGLIN. *Small Business Banking: A Guide to Marketing and Profits.* Rolling Meadows, IL: Bank Administration Institute, 1987.

GERSON, KATHLEEN. *Hard Choices: How Women Decide about Work, Career, and Motherhood.* Berkeley, CA: University of California Press, 1985.

GOLDBERG, GERTRUDE S., AND ELEANOR KREMEN. "The Feminization of Poverty: Only in America?" *Social Policy* (Spring 1987): 3–14.

GOODMAN, MARK. "Americans and Their Money." *Money*, November 1986, 159–66.

HARTMAN, CURTIS. "Fear of Franchising." *Inc.*, June 1987, 104–22.

HOFMEISTER, SALLIE. "On the Road to Ubiquity." *Venture*, November 1986, 48–53.

JOHNSON, KERRY L. *Peak Performance Selling: How to Increase Your Sales by 70 Percent within Six Weeks.* New York: Prentice-Hall, 1988.

KAGAN, JULIA, AND ROSALIND C. BARNETT. "Money Mastery." *Working Woman*, December 1986, 71–74.

KEY, WILSON BRYAN. *Subliminal Seduction.* New York: Signet, 1973.

LEVOY, ROBERT. *The Successful Professional Practice.* New York: Prentice-Hall, 1970.

LUXENBERG, STAN. *Roadside Empires: How the Chains Franchised America.* New York: Viking, 1985.

MCGRAYNE, SHARON. "Companies, Teams Clean Up through Trademark Licensing." *Crain's Detroit Business*, July 1986, 12.

OTTEN, ALAN L. "Women Continue to Outlive Men but the Female Edge Is Narrowing." *The Wall Street Journal*, June 5, 1985.

PETERS, THOMAS J., AND ROBERT H. WATERMAN, JR. *In Search of Excellence.* New York: Harper & Row, 1982.

PAOLA, SUZANNE. "What Lurks: A Survey of Consumers' Attitudes toward Their Money and toward Planners Tries Plucking Out the Heart of Their Mysteries." *Financial Planning*, June 1987, 105–12.

PRIDE, WILLIAM M., AND O. C. FERRELL. *Marketing*. 4th ed. Boston: Houghton Mifflin, 1985.

SEGLIN, JEFFREY L. *America's New Breed of Entrepreneurs*. Washington, DC: Acropolis, 1986.

SEGLIN, JEFFREY L., AND JEFFREY R. LAUTERBACH. *Personal Financial Planning in Banks: A Handbook for Decision Making*. Boston: Bankers, 1986.

SIVERD, BONNIE. "Love and Money in the 1980s." *Working Woman*, November 1985, 123–7, 161–2.

SIVERD, BONNIE. *The Working Woman Financial Advisor*. New York: Warner Books, 1987.

SMITH, KRISTINA. "Licensed Products: Fan Interest Is on the Rise." *The Sporting Goods Dealer*, June 1986, 62–65.

STOFFELS, KENNETH. "Merle Harmon's Plans Major Expansion." *The Business Journal* (Milwaukee), March 24, 1986.

WEITZMAN, LENORE. *The Divorce Revolution*. New York: Macmillan, 1987.

WHITTEMORE, MEG. "Franchising's Future." *Nation's Business*, February 1986, 47–53.

WYATT, LINDSAY K. *The Financial Planner's Guide to Publicity and Promotion: Techniques You Can Use to Market Your Financial Planning Practice*. Chicago, IL; Longman, 1987.

INDEX